Gordon Ramsay's
Great British Pub Food

Gordon Ramsay's

Great British Pub Food

Gordon Ramsay
Mark Sargeant

Food **Mark Sargeant** Text **Emily Quah**
Photographer **Emma Lee** Art Director **Patrick Budge**

Cook's notes

Spoon measures are level, unless otherwise specified:
1 tsp is equivalent to 5ml; 1 tbsp is equivalent to 15ml.

Use good-quality sea salt, freshly ground pepper and fresh herbs for the best flavour.

Use large eggs unless otherwise suggested, ideally organic or free-range. If you are pregnant or in a vulnerable health group, avoid dishes using raw egg whites or lightly cooked eggs.

Oven timings are for fan-assisted ovens. If using a conventional oven, increase the temperature by 15°C (1 Gas Mark). Individual ovens may vary in actual temperature by 10° from the setting, so it is important to know your oven. Use an oven thermometer to check its accuracy.

Timings are provided as guidelines, with a description of colour or texture where appropriate, but readers should rely on their own judgement as to when a dish is properly cooked.

HarperCollins*Publishers*
77–85 Fulham Palace Road Road,
Hammersmith, London W6 8JB
www.harpercollins.co.uk

Published by HarperCollins*Publishers* 2009

Text © 2009 Gordon Ramsay
Photography © 2009 Emma Lee

Art and design director: Patrick Budge
Project Editor: Janet Illsley
Photographer: Emma Lee
Food stylist: Mark Sargeant
Props stylist: Emma Thomas
Home economist: Emily Quah,
assisted by Cathryn Evans
Designer: Andrew Barron

A CIP catalogue record of this book is available from the British Library

ISBN 978-0-00-728982-0

Printed and bound in Great Britain by
Butler Tanner & Dennis Ltd, Frome, Somerset

Contents

Introduction

The great British Pub has played an important and unique role in British society right from Roman times, through the Middle Ages and up to the present day. It is a role that has changed, adapted and evolved as society has dictated, but the pub has always maintained its focus as the place to go – to relax, to celebrate, to mourn, to talk, to drink and, increasingly, to eat.

As a social chronicle, the pub has documented every cultural trend, often hand in hand with a legislative force that appears intent on protecting society. From controlling the hours during which pubs were allowed to open, to the most recent change, the banning of smoking, laws have tested the ingenuity of publicans to keep their doors open for business.

It might seem surprising that eating wasn't traditionally part of pub life. The earliest taverns may have supplied bread with the ale, but the concept of eating out had not been born. You ate at home and you went to the pub for your social needs. This was where you drank, smoked and sought entertainment through conversation. It catered for the social divide with public rooms and screened-off snugs where employers, the employed, the vicar, the widower and the retired could go, albeit often with a pricing hierarchy. A pint in the discrete snug with its frosted glass and privacy simply cost more.

The advent of television beckoned the end of the pub as the social epicentre. The concept of buying alcohol and taking it home was not lost on the evolving supermarket owners, who responded by stacking their shelves accordingly. Home now offered comfort with entertainment and without the restrictions of closing time or the risk of a drink-drive prosecution. The publican had to think hard in order to survive. Trade fell off. Real ale wasn't consumed at the same rate and suddenly the contents of barrels reached their 'best by' date before they had run dry. The brewers countered with a longer life offer, lager, which lived under pressure but it did not take away the problem of a diminished flow of alcohol.

Often the management, tenancy or ownership of a pub lay with a married couple. It was an ideal partnership in this social centre where the husband could attend to the barrel changing and control of his customers, while the wife busied herself with glass-washing and looking after the premises. If the business of serving beer was no longer what kept the bar team running around with the till ringing in the background, there had to be an opportunity for another offering.

There was now time and space for food. The concept of eating out was still in its infancy and the one overriding restriction was cost. The publican already had the premises, the seating and staff. All he had to do was arrange for a kitchen and a simple, good value bar menu to be made available. It was not only an opportunity to increase the flow of cash across the bar, but would, in time, bring back some of that lost wet trade. Moreover, a pub that began to make a name for itself for the quality of its food flourished. A restaurant was expensive and often made its new public feel uncomfortable. The pub had found a niche and suddenly there was the possibility for almost fifty thousand outlets to refocus their business.

The ban on smoking did pubs with grub no damage. On the contrary, it took away the one spoiler to eating good food in a convivial atmosphere. And there can be little doubt that any trade lost due to smokers who remained in their homes was regained as others now ventured forth to sample the food offerings of their local.

When we opened the Gordon Ramsay pubs in London, we wanted to give the public fantastic but casual food, served up alongside a few good pints and at a price that wouldn't break the bank. Not posh nosh, but classic British dishes that have stood the test of time. Our mantra has always been 'keep it simple and make it tasty' and that's exactly what we wanted to deliver in the pubs. We also wanted to bring back a few old-fashioned favourites, like cottage pie with Guinness, Lancashire hotpot and irresistibly sticky treacle tart.

This book brings to you dishes that have become pub classics. It offers simple, reasonably priced recipes that you can cook at home without fuss or complication. This is the food that has brought the British pub on to the culinary map.

BAR FOOD

Pint of prawns with mayo

Oysters with shallot vinegar

Devilled whitebait

Scotch eggs

Spiced nuts

Homemade pork scratchings

Angels and devils on horseback

Pan haggerty

Old-fashioned pork pies

Homemade crisps

Pickled quail's eggs

Wild boar sausage rolls

Pint of prawns with mayo

Walk into any pub and you are quite likely to find a pint of prawns with mayo on the bar menu. These tasty morsels from the Atlantic are perfect finger food to savour with a pint of light ale or a glass of dry white wine. As you peel off the shells from the prawns, suck the heads so you don't miss out on their amazing flavour.

To make the mayonnaise, put the egg yolks, wine vinegar, mustard and some salt and pepper into a blender or small food processor and whiz until the mixture is very thick and creamy. With the motor running, slowly trickle in the oil through the funnel in a steady stream. Add 1 tbsp water to help stabilize the emulsion, then taste and adjust the seasoning. (If the mayonnaise splits, transfer it to a bowl and start again. Whiz another egg yolk in the blender or processor until thick and then slowly blend in the split mixture; it should re-emulsify.)

Spoon the mayonnaise into individual dipping bowls and divide the prawns between four pint glasses. You might also want to put out an empty bowl for the shells. Any extra mayonnaise can be kept in a covered bowl in the fridge for up to 3 days.

SERVES 4
1–1.2kg cooked Atlantic
   prawns in shells

MAYONNAISE
2 large egg yolks
1 tsp white wine vinegar
1 tsp English mustard
sea salt and black pepper
300ml groundnut oil
   (or light olive oil)
1 tbsp water

Oysters with shallot vinegar

SERVES 4

2 shallots, peeled and
   finely chopped
120ml good-quality red
   wine vinegar (we use
   Cabernet Sauvignon)
12–16 very fresh native
   oysters

TO SERVE

rock salt
fresh seaweed
   (optional), to garnish

Sharing a platter of fresh oysters at the bar is a real treat. In London, our native oysters usually hail from Colchester or Whitstable, but they are gathered in various places around the British coast. Freshness is absolutely vital, so it helps to know your nearest source. Spanking fresh oysters taste of the sea.

Mix the shallots and wine vinegar together in a small bowl and leave to infuse for at least an hour. Spread a thick layer of rock salt on one or two serving platters and scatter over the seaweed, if available.

Shuck the oysters as you are about to serve them. To do so, hold an oyster, flat side upwards and level, in a folded tea towel in one hand. With the other hand, insert an oyster knife into the hinge of the oyster shell and wriggle it from side to side to cut through the hinge muscle. Push the knife further in and twist up to lift the top shell. Try not to tip out the juices as you do this. Hold the knife flat and slide it along the bottom shell to release the oyster, then flick off any pieces of broken shell. Place the oyster in its bottom shell on a serving plate. Repeat to shuck the rest. Serve immediately, with the shallot vinegar.

Devilled whitebait

SERVES 4–6

450g whitebait, thawed
  if frozen
170g plain flour
1 tsp cayenne pepper
sea salt and black pepper
150ml milk
groundnut or vegetable
  oil, for deep-frying

TO SERVE

extra cayenne pepper,
  to sprinkle (optional)
mayonnaise (see page
  246), for dipping
lemon wedges

These are a far cry from the soggy, overcooked whitebait we used to eat as kids whenever we were treated to a meal in a steakhouse. Freshly fried, these crisp, salty bites are lovely with a pint of ale. If using frozen whitebait, you may want to go easy on the extra salt as the tiny fish are usually soaked in brine before freezing.

Wash the whitebait, drain well and pat dry with kitchen paper. For the batter, in a bowl, mix 100g of the flour with the cayenne pepper and a pinch each of salt and pepper. Make a well in the middle and gradually whisk in the milk to make a smooth batter.

Heat an 8–10cm depth of oil in a deep-fryer or a heavy-based pan; the pan should be no more than half-full. The oil is ready when it reaches 190°C, or when a cube of bread dropped in turns golden brown in less than 40 seconds.

Deep-fry the whitebait in batches. Dip a handful into the remaining flour to coat, shaking off excess. Now dip the floured whitebait into the batter, then gently drop into the hot oil. Deep-fry for 1–2 minutes until golden and crisp. When you take them out of the oil, the whitebait should rustle as you shake them together. Try not to overcrowd the pan, as this will cause the temperature of the oil to drop too much.

Drain the whitebait on a tray lined with kitchen paper and keep warm in a low oven while you deep-fry the rest. If you wish, sprinkle on a little extra cayenne pepper. Serve while still crisp, with a bowl of mayonnaise and lemon wedges on the side.

Scotch eggs

MAKES 8

8 medium eggs, at room
    temperature
650g good-quality
    sausagemeat or 8–10
    butcher's sausages,
    removed from their
    skins
handful of flat-leaf
    parsley, finely chopped
4 sage leaves, finely
    chopped
1 tsp English mustard
    powder
grated zest of 1 lemon
sea salt and black pepper

TO ASSEMBLE

50g plain flour, sifted
2 large eggs, lightly
    beaten, for dipping
150g fine white
    breadcrumbs (made
    from one- or two-day
    old bread)
groundnut or vegetable
    oil, for deep-frying

TO SERVE

HP brown sauce

A good Scotch egg is determined by the quality of the sausagemeat and the cooking. The egg should be cooked until the yolk has just set and there should be no sign of a dark ring around the yolk, which indicates that it is over-cooked. These Scotch eggs can be made a couple of days in advance, but they are best enjoyed freshly cooked.

Bring a pan of water to the boil. Lower the eggs into the water and simmer for 8 minutes. Drain and cool under cold running water until the eggs no longer feel hot. Peel away the shells and set aside.

Put the sausagemeat into a bowl and add the parsley, sage, mustard powder, lemon zest and some seasoning. Mix together thoroughly, using one hand, then divide into 8 equal-sized balls. One at a time, flatten each sausagemeat ball on a piece of cling film to a circle, large enough to wrap around an egg. Place an egg in the middle, then draw up the ends of the cling film and massage the sausagemeat to cover the egg evenly. Repeat with the rest of the eggs and sausagemeat.

Have the flour, beaten eggs and breadcrumbs ready in three separate bowls. One at a time, roll each Scotch egg in the flour, then dip into the beaten egg and then into the breadcrumbs to coat. Dip into the egg and breadcrumbs once again for a really thorough coating. Repeat with the rest of the Scotch eggs.

Heat an 8cm depth of oil in a deep-fryer or heavy-based saucepan to 150°C. To test if it is ready for frying, drop a piece of bread into the oil; it should sizzle and turn light golden and crisp in less than a minute. Deep-fry the Scotch eggs two at a time. Lower them into the oil and fry for 4–5 minutes, turning once or twice to ensure they brown evenly.

Remove with a slotted spoon and drain on kitchen paper. Keep warm in a low oven while you fry the rest. Serve with HP sauce for dipping.

Spiced nuts

Along with potato crisps, salted nuts are essential bar nibbles. Our irresistible spiced nuts have a slight kick from cayenne pepper and a mild sweetness from caramelized sugar. They are incredibly more-ish, as you'll discover.

Preheat the oven to a low setting, about 140°C/Gas 1. Heat a large, heavy-based frying pan over a medium heat.

Mix the nuts, icing sugar, salt and cayenne pepper together in a wide bowl and grind over some black pepper. Tip the seasoned nuts into the hot pan. Sprinkle over a little water (about 1 tbsp) to help the sugar caramelize. Cook for 3–5 minutes, stirring or tossing the nuts around the pan constantly, until they start to release their oils and begin to take on some colour.

Tip the nuts onto a baking tray lined with greaseproof paper and spread them out in a single layer. Pop the tray into the low oven and leave the nuts to dry out for 30–40 minutes, tossing them a few times to make sure they colour evenly and don't burn.

Leave the nuts to cool completely. Store in an airtight container in a cool, dry place and use within a month.

SERVES 6–8

350g mixed whole, blanched (unsalted) nuts, such as cashews, hazelnuts and peanuts
2½ tbsp icing sugar
¾–1 tsp fine sea salt, to taste
1 tsp cayenne pepper, or to taste
black pepper

Homemade pork scratchings

SERVES 4–6

200g pork skins
(we generally use skins
from the belly)
coarse sea salt
groundnut or vegetable
oil, for deep-frying

We are probably one of very few nations in the world who eat snacks with hairs protruding from them! If you happen to be cooking pork belly and won't need the skin, remove and freeze it until you have time to prepare these savoury scratchings. Otherwise, your local butcher should be only too happy to sell you some pork skins. The crunchy pork scratchings keep well in an airtight container so you might want to double up the recipe.

Cut away or scrape off the excess fat from the pork skin, leaving an even layer attached to the skins, about 3mm thick. Rub or massage the skin with sea salt, place on a baking tray and chill in the fridge for 24–48 hours, to draw out excess moisture.

Dab off the beads of moisture with kitchen paper, then cut the skin into neat strips, about 1cm wide and 10cm long. Heat the oil in a deep-fryer or a heavy-based pan until it reaches about 120°C; the pan should be no more than half-full. Fry the skin strips in batches for about 8–9 minutes until they are cooked through and firm. Remove and drain.

Increase the heat and bring the oil to 195–200°C. Re-fry the pork skins in batches for another 2–3 minutes until they are golden brown and crisp; the skins may curl and bubble as they fry. Remove and drain on a tray lined with kitchen paper. The skins will continue to crisp up as they cool. When completely cooled, store in an airtight container unless you are serving the pork scratchings straight away.

Angels and devils
on horseback

These used to be offered on many bar menus, but you're more likely these days to find them served as canapés, or in the case of devils on horseback, with roast chicken, perhaps. A cinch to make, they are particularly appetizing with a cold lager or glass of white wine.

Preheat the grill to the highest setting and pre-soak 24 cocktail sticks in warm water (to prevent scorching under the grill).

For the angels, shuck the oysters (for technique, see page 16) and strain off the juices. (Save these to add to a fish soup or sauce.) Sprinkle each oyster lightly with white pepper and wrap in a piece of bacon. Fix securely with a cocktail stick. Place on a baking sheet, leaving a little space between each one, and drizzle over a little olive oil. Grill for about 3 minutes on each side, until the bacon is brown and crisp on top. Serve at once, or keep warm in a low oven while you make the devils.

For the devils, wrap each prune with a piece of bacon and cook in the same way as the angels. Serve piping hot.

SERVES 4

ANGELS
12 fresh native oysters
freshly ground white
  pepper
6 smoked streaky bacon
  rashers, derinded and
  halved lengthways
olive oil, to drizzle

DEVILS
12 soft d'Agen prunes
6 unsmoked streaky
  bacon rashers, derinded
  and halved lengthways

Pan haggerty

SERVES 4

600g firm, waxy
  potatoes, such as
  Desirée
3 large onions
100g strong cheddar
1½ tbsp olive oil
20g butter, melted
sea salt and black pepper

A pan haggerty consists of potatoes, onions and cheese – simple, comforting flavours you'd expect from a local bar. For a more intense flavour, use dripping from the weekend roast in place of butter. We also use gutsy, mature cheese, such as Montgomery or Westcombe cheddar from Somerset.

Peel and thinly slice the potatoes and onions, preferably using a mandoline for the potatoes. Coarsely grate the cheese and set aside.

Preheat the oven to 190°C/Gas 5. Heat the olive oil in a fairly small, ovenproof frying pan, about 20cm in diameter. Add the onions and sweat, stirring frequently, for 6–8 minutes until just softened. Transfer to a bowl and set aside.

Arrange a layer of potatoes over the base of the pan. Brush with some melted butter and season lightly with salt and pepper, then scatter over a thin layer of onions and cheese. Repeat layering the ingredients, making sure that you end up with a layer of cheese-topped potatoes.

Put the pan over a medium-high heat and cook for 2–3 minutes until the bottom layer of potatoes is golden brown. Transfer the pan to the oven and bake for 25–30 minutes, until the potatoes are tender when pierced with a small, sharp knife. The cheese topping should be golden; if not, increase the heat to 220°C/Gas 7 and bake for an extra 5 minutes or so.

Leave the pan haggerty to cool slightly for 5 minutes or so. Carefully slide it onto a warm plate, cut into slices and serve.

Old-fashioned pork pies

MAKES 8

HOT WATER CRUST PASTRY
250g plain flour
½ tsp fine sea salt
1 large egg
50g unsalted butter
50g lard
85ml water
1 medium egg yolk,
   lightly beaten with
   1 tbsp water, to glaze

FILLING
400g minced pork
   (roughly equal
   quantities of belly and
   shoulder meat)
250g sausagemeat
1 tbsp chopped parsley
1 tbsp chopped sage
finely grated zest of
   1 lemon
5 juniper berries, ground
   with a pinch of salt
pinch of allspice
sea salt and black pepper

Enjoy these adorable little pies warm or cold with piccalilli or pickled onions and a pint of ale.

To make the pastry, sift the flour and salt into a large bowl and make a well in the middle. Crack the egg into the well and sprinkle over some of the flour. Put the butter, lard and water into a small pan and heat gently until melted, then bring to the boil. Immediately pour around the edge of the flour and quickly stir together, using a butter knife, to combine. Knead the dough lightly until smooth; it will be quite soft at this stage. Wrap in cling film and chill for at least an hour until firm.

Meanwhile, for the filling, mix all the ingredients together, seasoning well. Divide into 8 portions, about 80g each, and roll into balls. Cut off one-third of the pastry for the pie lids, re-wrap and chill. Roll out the remaining pastry on a lightly floured work surface to the thickness of a £1 coin. Using a saucer, about 11cm in diameter, as a template, cut out 8 circles. Roll out the reserved pastry to the same thickness and cut out 7cm rounds for the lids, using a pastry cutter.

To assemble each pie, place a stuffing ball in the middle of a pastry base and flatten it slightly to get a flat base and straighter sides. Put a pastry lid on top. Brush the pastry base border with egg glaze, then draw up it up around the filling to meet the lid. Curl the edge of the lid up to meet the top inside edge of the pie case and pinch together to seal. Repeat with the other pies, then crimp the edges. Chill until firm.

Preheat the oven to 190°C/Gas 5. Place the pies on a baking sheet and make a hole in the centre of each lid with a skewer. Bake for 15 minutes, then reduce the setting to 170°C/Gas 3. Brush the pies evenly with egg glaze and bake for a further 10 minutes until cooked. To test, insert a skewer into the centre of a pie for a few seconds; it should feel hot to the touch as you remove it. Transfer the pies to a wire rack to cool.

Homemade crisps

Here you can experiment with different varieties of potato and other root vegetables, such as parsnips, carrots and beetroot. We love the flavour of waxy Charlotte potatoes. A touch of paprika or cayenne pepper gives them a slightly smoky sweet quality. The crisps will get soft if you leave them out for long, so store them in an airtight container until ready to serve.

Peel the potatoes and rinse well. Cut them into very thin slices, about 2mm thick, ideally using a mandoline. Rinse the potato slices under cold running water to remove the excess starch. Pat them dry using one or two clean tea towels, then spread the slices out on a baking tray to dry out further.

Heat an 8–10cm depth of oil in a deep-fryer or a heavy-based pan over a medium-high heat; the pan should be no more than one-third full. The oil is ready when it reaches 190°C, or when a cube of bread dropped in turns golden brown in less than 40 seconds. Fry the potatoes in batches. Add the slices to the pan a few at a time to prevent them from sticking together. Deep-fry for 3–4 minutes until golden and crisp, moving and turning the potatoes to ensure they colour evenly.

Remove with a slotted spoon, drain off excess oil and spread the crisps out on a tray lined with kitchen paper. Sprinkle with the cayenne and salt mix, then leave to cool completely. Store the crisps in an airtight container unless serving straight away.

SERVES 4

700g waxy potatoes, such as Desirée or Charlotte
groundnut or vegetable oil, for deep-frying
1 tsp cayenne pepper mixed with 1 tsp sea salt

Pickled quail's eggs

SERVES 4–6

24 quail's eggs, at room
  temperature
350ml white wine
  vinegar
125ml water
1½ tsp fine sea salt
1½ tsp cayenne pepper
6 black peppercorns
1 tsp mustard seeds
2 bay leaves
½ tsp allspice

Quintessential bar food, pickled eggs are like marmite – you either love them or hate them. But even today, you'll often find a jar of them lurking behind the counter in many pubs. This recipe uses dainty quail's eggs, which are easier to handle when you've got a drink in one hand.

Place the quail's eggs in a saucepan and add just enough water to cover. Bring to the boil and cook for 3 minutes, then drain and immerse in a bowl of cold water to cool quickly. When the eggs are cool enough to handle, peel and put them into clean, sterilized jars.

Meanwhile, put all the remaining ingredients into a non-reactive pan and bring to the boil. Remove from the heat and allow to cool slightly. Pour the spiced vinegar mixture over the eggs to cover completely, then seal the jars with tight-fitting lids. Refrigerate and leave for at least a week before eating.

Wild boar sausage rolls

SERVES 6

500g good-quality
  butter puff pastry
1½–2 tsp English
  mustard
6 thick good-quality
  wild boar sausages,
  about 450g (or use
  sausagemeat)
1 large egg yolk,
  beaten with 1 tsp water,
  to glaze
sesame seeds, to sprinkle

Sausage rolls are a great bar snack when you're after something a little more substantial with a drink, but not a full meal. This recipe is one of several versions we serve at the pubs, using fantastic wild boar sausagemeat and good-quality puff pastry. You can substitute any kind of sausage for the filling, but do try to get one with a higher meat/lower fat content, preferably from a good butcher.

Roll out the pastry on a floured surface to a large rectangle, about 3mm in thickness. Cut out 6 rectangles, about 10cm x 12cm (they should be just large enough to wrap around a sausage, so use one as a guide). Brush the pastry rectangles with a light coating of mustard.

Peel off the skins from the sausages. Lay a sausage along one longer side of a pastry rectangle and roll the pastry around it, overlapping the ends slightly and pressing them lightly to seal. Put the sausage roll, seam side down, on a baking sheet lined with greaseproof paper. Repeat to make the rest of the sausage rolls, leaving some space between them to allow for expansion on cooking. Brush the tops with some of the beaten egg and rest in the fridge for at least 20 minutes.

Preheat the oven to 200°C/Gas 6. Brush the sausage rolls once again with the egg and sprinkle the tops with sesame seeds. Bake for 25–30 minutes until the pastry is golden brown and the sausages are cooked through. Transfer to a wire rack and leave to cool slightly before serving. Although you can enjoy them cold, these sausage rolls are best served warm and freshly baked.

SAVOURIES WITH TOAST

Scotch woodcock

Creamed haddock and pickled walnuts on toast

Anchovies on toast with poached egg and spinach

St. George's mushrooms on toast

Soft herring roes on toast

Potted duck

Potted crab

Potted shrimps with toast

Potted hough

Devilled kidneys on toast

Sardines and tomatoes on toast

Roasted bone marrow with caper and herb dressing

Welsh rabbit

Scotch woodcock

SERVES 4

14 anchovy fillets in oil

50g butter, softened,
 plus a few knobs of
 cold butter

black pepper

4 large eggs

pinch of cayenne pepper

4 slices of white or
 brown bread

1 tsp capers, rinsed and
 drained

Back in the days when gentlemen's clubs were prevalent, small portions of savouries on toast took the place of sweet puddings as an alternate way to end a meal – much like our modern-day cheese and biscuits. Scotch woodcock is one such dish. Simply scrambled eggs with anchovies on toast, it couldn't be easier to make. The tradition is to adorn the scrambled eggs with two anchovies laid in the shape of a cross to symbolize the Scottish flag.

Finely chop or mash 6 anchovy fillets and mix with the softened butter and a generous grinding of black pepper. Set aside.

Melt a few knobs of butter in a saucepan. In a bowl, whisk the eggs together with a pinch of cayenne, then pour into the pan and stir slowly over a gentle heat until the mixture begins to thicken. Remove the pan from the heat and continue to stir the eggs until they are scrambled and creamy.

Meanwhile, toast the bread slices. Spread them generously with the anchovy butter and place on warm serving plates. Add the capers to the scrambled eggs, then quickly spoon on top of the toasts. Garnish each serving with two crossed anchovies and serve.

Creamed haddock
and pickled walnuts on toast

Enriching smoked haddock with cream gives the fish a lovely silky texture for this savoury base. Pickled walnuts add a sweet tang that cuts through the richness perfectly.

Bring a wide, shallow pan of water to a simmer and add the haddock fillets, skin side down. Poach gently for 3–4 minutes until the flesh is just cooked and flakes easily. Using a fish slice, carefully transfer the fish to a plate and leave to cool for a few minutes. While still warm, flake the fish, discarding the skin and removing any pin-bones.

Heat the olive oil in a pan, add the leek and sauté for 4–5 minutes, until soft. Pour in the cream and simmer until it has reduced slightly and thickened. Fold through the flaked fish. Add a generous grinding of black pepper and taste for seasoning. (You probably won't need to add salt, as smoked haddock is usually quite salty.) Remove from the heat and keep warm.

Toast the bread slices and place on warm plates. Pile the smoked haddock mixture generously onto the toasts and arrange the pickled walnut slices on top. Serve at once.

SERVES 4
450g smoked haddock fillets
1½ tbsp olive oil
1 large leek, white part only, trimmed and finely chopped
300ml double cream
black pepper
4 slices of thick country bread
3–4 pickled walnuts, drained and finely sliced

Anchovies on toast

with poached egg and spinach

This simple but delicious combination of salty anchovies, creamy poached eggs and earthy spinach atop crunchy toast makes a fantastic weekend brunch.

First, poach the eggs in advance. Bring a pan of water to a simmer. Add a few drops of vinegar and swirl with a slotted spoon to create a whirlpool effect. Cook the eggs two at a time: crack one into a small bowl and gently slide into the centre of the whirlpool; repeat with another egg. Poach for about 3 minutes until the whites are set but the yolk is still runny in the middle. Remove each egg with a slotted spoon and slide into a bowl of cold water to stop the cooking process. Repeat to cook the other eggs.

When you are ready to serve, heat the olive oil in a wide pan. When hot, add the spinach leaves and stir over a high heat until the spinach has just wilted. Remove from the heat and season well with salt, pepper and a grating of nutmeg. Meanwhile, toast the bread slices and reheat the eggs in a pan of gently simmering water for a minute.

Place the toasts on warm serving plates and pile the wilted spinach on top. Drape the anchovies over the spinach. One at a time, remove the poached eggs from the pan with a slotted spoon. Dab the bottom of the spoon with kitchen paper to soak up any water, then place the egg on top of the anchovies. Grind over a little black pepper and serve at once.

SERVES 4

4 large eggs
few drops of white wine or cider vinegar
1 tbsp olive oil, plus extra to drizzle
300g spinach leaves, washed and dried
sea salt and black pepper
nutmeg, to grate
4 slices of brown soda bread
12 anchovy fillets in oil, halved if large

St. George's mushrooms on toast

SERVES 4

250g St. George's
  mushrooms, cleaned
40g butter
sea salt and black pepper
squeeze of lemon juice
few oregano sprigs,
  leaves only, chopped
small bunch of flat-leaf
  parsley, leaves only,
  chopped
4 slices of brown or
  Granary bread

Even though it is not so well known among fungi, the St. George's mushroom can take pride of place amongst the finest wild mushrooms, as its firm, meaty texture and distinctive woody flavour are hard to beat. This recipe also works well with portobello or chestnut mushrooms.

Slice the mushrooms thinly. Melt the butter in a wide frying pan and, as soon as it begins to foam, tip in the mushrooms. Sprinkle with a little salt and pepper and fry, stirring occasionally, over a high heat for a few minutes. Add a squeeze of lemon juice and fry the mushrooms until lightly browned and any moisture has cooked off. Season well and toss in the herbs.

Meanwhile, toast the bread. Divide the mushrooms between the hot toasts and serve at once.

Soft herring roes on toast

SERVES 4

450g herring roes
1½ tbsp olive oil
sea salt and black pepper
75g butter, in pieces
4 slices of white or
 brown bread
handful of flat-leaf
 parsley, leaves only,
 chopped
squeeze of lemon juice
lemon wedges, to serve

For those who have yet to try herring roes, they have a surprising creaminess and delicious taste that is further enhanced with a little nutty butter and lemon juice. Pile them on freshly toasted crusty bread for a great balance of flavours and textures.

Rinse the herring roes and pat dry on kitchen paper. Heat a large frying pan and add the olive oil. Season the roes with salt and pepper and fry in the hot pan for 2–3 minutes until lightly golden. Add the butter and allow to melt. Spoon the foaming butter over the roes as they cook for another minute or so, to encourage them to brown. Meanwhile, toast the bread.

Remove the herring roes from the heat, add the chopped parsley and a squeeze of lemon juice and toss through quickly. Check the seasoning.

Put a slice of toast on each warm plate and top with the herring roes, spooning over any buttery pan juices. Serve immediately, with lemon wedges on the side.

Potted duck

SERVES 4–6
2 duck legs, about
  300g each
2 large garlic cloves,
  peeled and chopped
few thyme sprigs
sea salt and black pepper
300g duck fat, melted
60g pistachio nuts,
  toasted and roughly
  chopped

TO SERVE
plenty of sourdough
  bread slices, freshly
  toasted
pickled onions and
  cornichons

Pistachios help to cut the richness of this tasty spread, as do the accompanying pickled onions and cornichons.

Preheat the oven to 150°C/Gas 2. Put the duck legs, skin side up, into a roasting tin in which they fit snugly and scatter over the garlic, thyme and seasoning. Pour over the duck fat to cover. Roast for 2–2½ hours until the meat is very tender and falls off the bone. Cool slightly, then lift the duck legs onto a plate, reserving the fat. Shred or finely chop the meat, discarding the skin. Place the meat in a bowl. Strain the fat through a fine sieve; set aside.

Add the pistachios to the duck and toss to mix, moistening with a little duck fat and seasoning generously to taste. Divide the mixture among 4–6 small jars or ramekins. Press down with the back of a spoon and pour over a thin layer of duck fat to cover. Chill until set.

Take the potted duck out of the fridge 30–40 minutes before serving to soften it slightly, so it can be spread. Serve with warm toast, pickled onions and cornichons.

Potted crab

This is a lovely way to serve crab, as you can really savour the flavour with every mouthful.

Melt 100g of the butter in a heavy-based saucepan, add the shallots and sweat over a medium-low heat, stirring occasionally, for 6–8 minutes until they are soft but not browned. Stir in the spices, then the anchovy paste and sherry. Cook for a few more minutes until the alcohol from the sherry has evaporated.

Add the white and brown crabmeat to the spicy butter and stir to combine. Season well with salt, pepper and lemon juice. Stir over a low heat until the crabmeat is warmed through, then immediately take off the heat.

Divide the mixture between 4–6 small ramekins and press down lightly to level the tops. Melt the remaining 50g butter in the same pan and spoon a thin layer over the crabmeat to cover. Cool and chill until set.

Take the ramekins out of the fridge about 30 minutes before serving to allow the butter to soften. Serve with lots of warm toast.

SERVES 4–6

150g unsalted butter, cubed
2 shallots, peeled and finely chopped
$\frac{1}{3}$ tsp cayenne pepper
$\frac{1}{3}$ tsp ground mace
$\frac{1}{3}$ tsp freshly grated nutmeg
1 anchovy fillet in oil, finely crushed to a paste
3 tbsp sherry
375g white crabmeat
75g brown crabmeat
sea salt and black pepper
2 tsp lemon juice, or to taste

TO SERVE

plenty of brown or Granary bread slices, freshly toasted

Potted shrimps with toast

SERVES 6

150g unsalted butter, cubed

2 shallots, peeled and finely chopped

50ml medium dry sherry

⅓ tsp cayenne pepper, or to taste

⅓ tsp ground mace

⅓ tsp freshly grated nutmeg, plus extra to finish

570ml pot Morecambe Bay brown shrimps

sea salt and black pepper

2 tsp lemon juice

TO SERVE

plenty of white or brown bread slices, freshly toasted

Brown shrimps from Morecambe Bay are renowned for their nutty taste and delicate texture. They are caught and cooked straight away in seawater on the boats, to preserve their fantastic flavour. Use ordinary brown shrimps if you can't get them.

Melt 120g of the butter in a heavy-based saucepan, add the shallots and sweat over a medium-low heat, stirring occasionally, for 6–8 minutes until they are soft but not browned. Add the sherry and simmer until you can no longer detect an aroma of alcohol. Tip in the spices and stir well. Cook for 2–3 minutes, stirring frequently.

Reduce the heat slightly, add the shrimps and stir to coat in the spicy butter. Taste and adjust the seasoning, adding a little salt and pepper, and the lemon juice. Once the shrimps are warmed through, remove the pan from the heat.

Spoon the shrimps and butter into six small ramekins and press down gently with the back of a spoon. Melt the remaining butter in the pan you cooked the shrimps in. Spoon a thin layer of clear butter over the potted shrimps to cover. Grate over a little nutmeg, then leave to cool completely. Chill until the butter has set.

Remove the potted shrimps from the fridge about 30 minutes before serving, to allow the butter to soften. Serve with plenty of warm toast, and perhaps a sharply dressed watercress salad.

Potted hough

SERVES 4

900g shin of beef on the
bone (ask your butcher
to crack the bone)
1 large carrot, peeled and
cut into large chunks
1 leek, trimmed and cut
into large chunks
1 onion, trimmed and cut
into large chunks
2 bay leaves
¼–½ tsp cayenne
pepper, to taste
½ tsp allspice
½ tsp black peppercorns
1 mace blade
sea salt and black pepper
handful of flat-leaf
parsley, leaves only,
chopped

TO SERVE

sourdough bread, freshly
toasted, or country
bread slices
piccalilli or pickled
gherkins

Hough is the Scottish name for shin of beef on the bone, an inexpensive flavoursome joint with a little more fat than most other beef cuts. Here it is braised until tender, then the meat is taken off the bone, shredded and mixed with the reduced stock prior to potting. It is not essential to cover the potted meat with a layer of fat, but it is best consumed within 4–5 days.

Place the beef in a large cooking pot and add enough cold water to cover. Bring to the boil, then reduce the heat to a simmer and skim off any froth or scum that rises to the surface. Continue to skim until the liquid is pretty much clear, then add the flavouring vegetables, bay leaves, spices and seasoning. Partially cover the pan and simmer very gently over a very low heat for 4–4½ hours until the beef is meltingly tender, skimming off any scum from time to time.

When the beef is ready, remove the pan from the heat and allow the beef to cool in the liquor. When cool enough to handle, lift out the beef and shred the meat from the bone. Put into a large bowl, cover and set aside.

Strain the stock through a fine sieve into another pan. Boil steadily for 15–20 minutes or until reduced by three-quarters, to about 250–300ml. Season the reduced stock generously to taste, then pour over the shredded meat to bind. Taste and adjust the seasoning once again, and mix in the chopped parsley. Divide between four small ramekins, packing the meat in well. Cool completely, then chill until set.

Remove from the fridge about 30 minutes before serving. To unmould, dip a ramekin in a bowl of hot water for a few seconds, then invert and tip out onto a plate. Serve with warm sourdough toasts or rustic country bread and piccalilli or pickled gherkins on the side.

Devilled kidneys on toast

Lamb's kidneys have a fairly strong and distinctive taste, which can take a slightly spicy, sweet and sour devil sauce. This savoury is equally suitable for a weekend brunch or a fast, light supper.

First, prepare the devil sauce. Put all the ingredients into a small saucepan, add some salt and pepper and bring to the boil. Let bubble for about 15–20 minutes until reduced right down to a syrupy sauce that is thick enough to lightly coat the back of a spoon.

Meanwhile, to prepare the kidneys, cut them in half lengthways and carefully remove the white sinewy cores with the tip of a small knife.

When you are ready to serve, heat a frying pan and add the butter. Season the kidneys with salt and pepper and add to the butter as it starts to sizzle. Fry for 2 minutes until browned, then turn the kidneys over and cook the other side for a minute. Add the sauce and spoon it over the kidneys to baste them as they cook for another minute. Meanwhile, toast the bread.

Place a slice of warm toast on each warm plate and top with the devilled kidneys. Spoon over any remaining sauce from the pan and serve at once, sprinkled with some chopped parsley if you like.

SERVES 4
8 lamb kidneys, rinsed
few knobs of butter
sea salt and black pepper

DEVIL SAUCE
375ml medium dry
  sherry
4 tbsp white wine
  vinegar
2 tbsp redcurrant jelly
1 tbsp Worcestershire
  sauce
¾ tsp cayenne pepper,
  or to taste
2 tbsp dry English
  mustard

TO SERVE
4 thick slices of country
  bread
handful of flat-leaf
  parsley, leaves chopped
  (optional)

Sardines and tomatoes on toast

SERVES 4

6 small, very fresh
  sardines, filleted
500g cherry tomatoes
  on the vine
olive oil, to drizzle
few thyme sprigs, leaves
  stripped
2 garlic cloves, peeled
  and finely sliced
sea salt and black pepper
8 thick slices of Granary
  or sourdough bread,
  to serve

Using vine-ripened cherry tomatoes and the freshest of sardines, this is an elegant, grown-up version of tinned sardines in tomato sauce on toast – a family favourite when we were kids.

Check the sardine fillets for any pin-bones and remove with tweezers. (Tiny bones are fine to eat and can be left in.) Pat dry with kitchen paper and chill until ready to cook. Preheat the oven to 200°C/Gas 6.

Lay the tomatoes on a baking tray and drizzle with a little olive oil. Scatter over the thyme, garlic and a pinch each of salt and pepper. Roast for 8–10 minutes until the skins have burst and the flesh is soft.

Shortly before the tomatoes will be ready, season the sardines and lay them, skin side up, on a lightly oiled baking tray. Drizzle with olive oil and bake for 3–4 minutes until they feel just firm when lightly pressed.

Meanwhile, toast the bread. Put a slice of toast on each warm plate and lay the roasted tomatoes on top. Arrange the sardine fillets over the tomatoes, sprinkle with a little salt and serve immediately.

Roasted bone marrow
with caper and herb dressing

SERVES 4

12 short pieces of veal
  marrowbones
  (or 8 longer lengths)
sea salt and black pepper

**CAPER AND HERB
DRESSING**

large handful of flat-leaf
  parsley, leaves only,
  chopped
few oregano sprigs,
  leaves only
2 shallots, peeled and
  roughly chopped
2 tsp capers, rinsed and
  drained
2 tsp Dijon or English
  mustard
1 tbsp cider or white
  wine vinegar
4 tbsp extra virgin olive
  oil
few dashes of Tabasco
  sauce (optional)

TO SERVE

about 8 slices of
  sourdough bread
1 lemon, cut into wedges

Bone marrow has recently regained popularity, largely due to the efforts of chefs like Fergus Henderson, who often serves it at his restaurant, St. John's, in London. Our version pairs rich marrow with a punchy caper and herb dressing. If you're feeling indulgent, serve the buttery marrow on brioche toasts instead of sourdough.

Preheat the oven to 190°C/Gas 5. Lightly season both ends of the marrowbones with salt and pepper and place in a roasting tin. Roast for about 20 minutes until the marrow is soft and will come away from the bone when you prod it lightly. Take care not to over-roast or the marrow will melt into an oily mass.

To make the dressing, put all the ingredients into a food processor and pulse until the mixture forms a rough paste. Check the seasoning, then spoon into small individual serving bowls.

When the marrowbones are almost ready, toast the bread. Stand the marrowbones upright on warm serving plates with the toasted sourdough, lemon wedges and bowls of caper and herb dressing on the side.

Welsh rabbit

For this classic savoury, we use farmhouse cheese, stout and the ultimate British condiment, Worcestershire sauce.

Melt the butter in a pan over a low heat. Whisk in the flour and cook, stirring, for 2–3 minutes. Gradually stir in the milk, keeping the mixture smooth, then add the cheese and stir until melted. Take off the heat. Stir in the Guinness, Worcestershire sauce, mustard and seasoning to taste. Transfer to a bowl and let cool, then mix in the egg yolks.

Heat the grill to its highest setting. Toast the bread on both sides, then spread a layer of cheese mixture on top and grill for a few minutes until the topping is bubbling and golden brown. Serve at once.

SERVES 4–6

30g butter
30g plain flour
150ml hot milk
55g mature cheddar, grated
50ml Guinness
1 tsp Worcestershire sauce
1 tsp Dijon or English mustard
sea salt and black pepper
2 large egg yolks
4–6 thick slices of white bread

SOUPS AND BROTHS

Cock-a-leekie soup

Chilled minted pea soup

White onion and cheddar soup

Roasted tomato and marrow soup

London particular

Fennel and roasted red pepper soup

Mulligatawny

Cullen skink

Potato, bacon and oyster soup

Welsh mutton broth

Hodge podge soup

Cock-a-leekie soup

SERVES 6–8

1 chicken, about 1.5kg,
  jointed
sea salt and black pepper
1 bouquet garni (bay leaf,
  few thyme and parsley
  sprigs, tied together)
1.5–2 litres chicken stock
  (see page 243), or water
5 large leeks, about 500g
  in total, trimmed
200g cooked rice
200g soft pitted prunes

This winter warmer is traditionally served as a starter at Scottish holiday feasts, including Hogmanay and Burn's Night. As the name suggests, chicken and leeks are the key ingredients, along with prunes. We like the mild sweetness these add to the light and savoury broth, but you can leave them out if you prefer.

Rub the chicken joints with salt and pepper and place in a large cooking pot with the bouquet garni and stock. If the stock doesn't quite cover the chicken, top up with cold water. Add a generous pinch each of salt and pepper and bring the liquid to a simmer. Skim off any froth or scum that rises to the surface. Turn the heat to the lowest setting, partially cover the pan and simmer gently for 30 minutes; the surface of the liquid should barely move.

In the meantime, slice the leeks on the diagonal into 1–2cm wide pieces. Add them to the pan and simmer for 30 minutes until the chicken is tender throughout.

Lift the chicken out of the stock and leave until cool enough to handle. Meanwhile, add the rice and prunes to the stock and simmer for another 15–20 minutes. Remove the bouquet garni.

Shred the chicken meat, discarding the skin and bones, then return to the stock to warm through. Taste and adjust the seasoning. Ladle the soup into warm soup plates to serve.

Chilled minted pea soup

Effortless to prepare, this vibrant soup makes a refreshing summer starter. If preferred, it can be served hot.

Heat the olive oil in a pan. Add the shallots, season and sweat over a medium heat, stirring occasionally, for 5–6 minutes until they begin to soften but not colour. Add the peas and pour in the stock; it should just cover the peas. Simmer for a few minutes until the peas are tender. Drop in the mint and immediately take off the heat.

Using a slotted spoon, take out a spoonful of peas for the garnish. In batches if necessary, blend the soup using a hand-held stick blender (or a regular blender) until smooth. Adjust the seasoning generously, as the flavours will be muted when cold. Pour into a bowl set over another bowl half-filled with ice to cool quickly, stirring occasionally. Chill for at least 2 hours before serving, topped with the reserved peas and a grinding of pepper.

SERVES 4

2 tbsp olive oil, plus extra to drizzle

2 large shallots, peeled and finely chopped

sea salt and black pepper

500g frozen peas, thawed

about 600ml hot chicken stock (see page 243)

small bunch of mint, leaves only

White onion and cheddar soup

In the spring, we use new season's onions to lend a wonderful sweetness to this lovely, creamy onion soup. A strong piquant cheese, such as Montgomery cheddar with its slight edge, contrasts the sweetness perfectly.

Melt the butter in a large pan. Add the onions and sprinkle with some salt and pepper. Cook, stirring frequently, over a medium heat for about 7–10 minutes until the onions are soft and translucent but not browned. Add the garlic, bay and thyme leaves, and cook for another 3–4 minutes.

Pour in the stock, bring to a gentle simmer, cover the pan and cook for 10 minutes or until the onions are very soft. Remove from the heat and discard the bay leaves. Purée the soup, using a hand-held stick blender (or a regular blender) until smooth. For a very smooth texture if preferred, pass the puréed soup through a fine sieve.

Return the soup to the pan. Add the milk and cream and slowly return to a gentle simmer. Stir in the grated cheese and season well to taste. Serve in warm bowls, with some warm buttery scones or crusty bread on the side.

SERVES 4

20g butter
900g white onions, peeled and sliced
sea salt and black pepper
2 garlic cloves, peeled and finely crushed
2 bay leaves
few thyme sprigs, leaves stripped
300ml chicken stock (see page 243)
200ml whole milk
75ml double cream
100g strong cheddar, such as Montgomery, grated

Roasted tomato and marrow soup

SERVES 4

1kg vine-ripened
  tomatoes, about 12
1 marrow, about 1kg
olive oil, to drizzle
few thyme sprigs, leaves
  stripped
3 large garlic cloves,
  peeled and thinly sliced
2 tsp caster sugar
sea salt and black pepper
small bunch of basil,
  leaves only, roughly
  chopped
300ml hot chicken or
  vegetable stock
  (see page 243)
1–2 tsp good-quality
  balsamic vinegar

Marrow is popular with gardeners but much less so with cooks, probably because its watery texture is something of a challenge. Roasting the vegetable concentrates the flavour and makes it a natural partner for roasted tomatoes in this summery soup. Serve it simply with a drizzle of good olive oil, or crumble some goat's cheese on top and scatter over a handful of crunchy garlicky croûtons.

Preheat the oven to 200°C/Gas 6. Halve the tomatoes and arrange, cut side up, on a baking tray. Peel, halve and deseed the marrow, then cut into 1.5cm cubes and spread out on another baking tray. Drizzle both generously with olive oil, then scatter over the thyme leaves, garlic, sugar and some salt and pepper. Toss the marrow cubes to ensure that they are well coated. Roast the tomatoes and marrows for 30–40 minutes, until they are soft and slightly caramelized, giving the marrows a stir halfway through.

As soon as they are cooked, purée the vegetables in a blender with the basil leaves and hot stock; do this in two batches if necessary and make sure you tip in all the flavourful juices. For a very smooth texture if preferred, pass the puréed soup through a fine sieve.

Transfer the soup to a pan and reheat gently. Taste and adjust the seasoning with a little balsamic vinegar, salt and pepper. Serve in warm bowls drizzled with a little olive oil.

London particular

During the industrial revolution, London was often blanketed in a thick heavy fog – referred to as a 'pea souper' and this is how this soup acquired its name. It is typically made with boiled unsmoked gammon, but we prefer to use a smoked ham hock to give the soup an intense and smoky base flavour. The croûtons add a contrasting crunch, but you can omit them if you prefer.

Drain the ham hock, rinse under cold running water and place in a large pan. Add the onion, carrot, celery, peppercorns and bouquet garni, then pour in the water to cover. Bring to a simmer and skim off the scum and froth that rises to the surface. Simmer gently, topping up with boiling water as necessary, for 2½–3 hours until the ham is tender and comes away from the bone easily.

Lift out the ham and let cool slightly. Strain the stock and return to the pan. Drain the split peas, add to the pan and simmer for 1½–2 hours until soft. In the meantime, shred the ham and discard the bone.

Purée the soup using a hand-held stick blender (or a regular blender) until smooth. Return to the pan to reheat. If the soup is too thick, add a little boiling water to dilute; or, if it is not thick enough, simmer until reduced to the required consistency. Taste and adjust the seasoning. Return the ham pieces to the soup and reheat just before serving.

To make the croûtons, cut the French stick into small bite-sized pieces. Heat the olive oil and butter in a small frying pan. When hot, add the bread pieces and toss in the foaming butter and oil for 3 minutes or so, until golden brown and crisp. Remove with a slotted spoon and drain well on kitchen paper.

Divide the hot soup among warm bowls and scatter a few croûtons and parsley leaves on top. Hand the rest of the croûtons round separately.

SERVES 4–6

1 smoked ham hock, about 1kg, soaked in plenty of cold water overnight
1 large onion, peeled and halved
1 large carrot, peeled and cut into 3 pieces
1 celery stick, trimmed and cut into 3 pieces
1 tsp white peppercorns
1 bouquet garni (1 bay leaf, few thyme or parsley sprigs, tied together)
1½–2 litres water
300g dried split green peas, soaked overnight
sea salt and black pepper

CROÛTONS

1 day-old thin French stick
4 tbsp olive oil
30g butter

TO GARNISH

flat-leaf parsley leaves

Fennel and roasted red pepper soup

SERVES 4

4 red peppers
1 large fennel bulb,
  trimmed (fronds
  reserved if intact)
1 large potato, peeled
2 tbsp olive oil, plus extra
  to drizzle
1 tsp fennel seeds
1½ tsp caster sugar
sea salt and black pepper
splash of Pernod
  (optional)
500ml chicken or
  vegetable stock
  (see page 243)
75ml soured cream
  (or double cream)
few dill sprigs (optional),
  to garnish

This is another fantastic soup for the summer, which you can serve either hot or chilled as you prefer. Roasting the peppers intensifies their flavour but if you are short of time, use a jar or two of ready roasted peppers – available from most supermarkets.

Heat the grill to its highest setting. Quarter the peppers lengthways and remove the seeds. Arrange on a sturdy baking sheet, skin side up, and place under the hot grill for about 5 minutes, until the skins char and blacken. Tip the pepper pieces into a bowl, immediately cover with cling film and leave them to steam for a few minutes; this helps to lift the skins.

Meanwhile, dice the fennel and potato. Heat the olive oil in a wide, heavy-based pan and sauté the fennel for 3–4 minutes until it begins to colour. Add the potato, fennel seeds, sugar and a pinch each of salt and pepper. Stir frequently over a high heat for another 4–5 minutes. If using, add the Pernod and let bubble for a few minutes. Pour in the stock, bring to a simmer and cook for 10–15 minutes until the vegetables are very soft.

Once the peppers are cool enough to handle, peel away the skins and chop the flesh into small dice. Add half of the peppers to the soup, then purée using a hand-held stick blender (or a regular blender) until very smooth. Stir in the cream and remaining chopped peppers, then taste and adjust the seasoning. Reheat as necessary. Ladle into bowls and garnish with the reserved fennel fronds or dill sprigs.

Mulligatawny

Originating during colonial times, this soup has retained its popularity to this day. We like to serve it at our pub, The Narrow, which is located near East India Docks – once the landing port for exotic spices shipped in from the Far East. This mildly spiced soup may very well have expanded the English palate and ignited our love of Indian curries.

Melt the butter in a pan, add the onions with some seasoning and sweat for 3–4 minutes, until they begin to soften. Stir in the tomato purée, curry powder and flour, and cook, stirring frequently, for 2 minutes until fragrant. Add the ginger and apple, and stir over a high heat for a few minutes.

Pour in the stock, stirring and scraping the bottom of the pan with a wooden spoon to deglaze. Add the coconut milk and bring back to a simmer. Let bubble gently until reduced slightly and thickened. Add the rice and simmer for another 3–4 minutes. Season generously with salt and pepper to taste.

Ladle the soup into warm bowls and garnish with a swirl of soured cream and a scattering of coriander leaves.

SERVES 4

25g butter
2 large onions, peeled and chopped
sea salt and black pepper
3 tbsp tomato purée
2–3 tsp mild curry powder, to taste
2 tbsp plain flour
2–3 tbsp grated fresh root ginger
1 green apple, peeled and grated
400ml chicken stock (see page 243)
400ml tin coconut milk
150g cooked rice

TO SERVE

3–4 tbsp soured cream (or double cream)
small handful of coriander leaves

Cullen skink

This is a comforting soup that can be served either as a starter or a light lunch with plenty of crusty bread. It hails from the village of Cullen on the northeast coast of Scotland where Finnan haddie is readily available. This prized fish lends a wonderful smoky flavour to the creamy potato soup. If you can't get hold of it, then use any undyed smoked haddock.

Lay the smoked haddock fillets, skin side up, in a wide, shallow pan. Pour the milk over the fish to cover and add the bay leaves. Bring the milk to a gentle simmer and poach the fish for 3–4 minutes until it feels firm when lightly pressed. Remove the pan from the heat and set aside to infuse for 5 minutes.

Melt the butter in a large pan and sauté the shallots and garlic until soft, about 8–10 minutes. Meanwhile, peel the potatoes and cut into small dice. Add to the pan and cook for about 10 minutes, stirring occasionally, until lightly golden.

In the meantime, lift the haddock fillets out of the milk. While still warm, flake the flesh, discarding the skin and any bones you come across. Strain the milk over the shallots and potatoes, then pour in the stock and bring to a simmer. Cook gently for about 10–15 minutes until the potatoes are soft.

Add a quarter of the flaked haddock to the soup followed by the cream and remove from the heat. Using a hand-held stick blender (or a regular blender), blend until smooth. Reheat the soup and add the rest of the flaked haddock to warm through. Season with salt and pepper to taste.

Serve in warm bowls, topped with a little drizzle of olive oil and a sprinkling of parsley leaves, with some crusty bread on the side.

SERVES 4–6

500g undyed smoked haddock fillets, preferably Finnan haddie

500ml whole milk

2 bay leaves

20g butter

2 banana shallots (or 4–5 regular ones), peeled and finely chopped

2 large garlic cloves, peeled and finely chopped

600g waxy potatoes, such as Desirée or La Ratte

500ml chicken stock (see page 243) or fish stock (see page 245)

100ml double cream

sea salt and black pepper

olive oil, to drizzle (optional)

flat-leaf parsley leaves, to garnish

Potato, bacon and oyster soup

2 tbsp olive oil
6 smoked streaky bacon
   rashers, derinded and
   chopped
2 large onions, peeled
   and finely chopped
600g waxy potatoes,
   such as Desirée or
   Charlotte, peeled and
   diced
100ml dry white wine
650ml chicken stock
   (see page 243)
100g smoked oysters
   (or smoked mussels)
3–4 tbsp double cream
12 fresh native oysters
black pepper
squeeze of lemon juice,
   to taste
handful of flat-leaf
   parsley, chopped

Bacon and oysters are a classic combination. In times past, oysters were not regarded as a luxury ingredient to serve with Champagne. On the contrary, cooks added oysters to bulk up soups, stews and pie fillings. This soup was most likely thought of as a peasant dish, made with cheap but flavourful ingredients... how times have changed.

Heat the olive oil in a pan over a medium-high heat. Add the bacon and fry, stirring occasionally, for 4–5 minutes until it begins to colour. Add the onions and potatoes and stir frequently for another 5–6 minutes until the onions begin to soften.

Pour in the wine and let bubble until reduced right down. Pour in the stock and return to a simmer, then add the smoked oysters. Simmer for another 10–15 minutes until the potatoes are soft.

Ladle two-thirds of the soup into a blender and whiz until smooth. Pour back into the pan and stir well to mix. Add the cream and bring back to a simmer.

Shuck the fresh oysters (for technique, see page 16), saving and straining the juices. Tip the oysters and strained juices into the soup. Simmer for a minute, then taste and adjust the seasoning with a little black pepper and lemon juice. (You probably don't need to add any extra salt as the bacon and oysters are quite salty.) Ladle into warm bowls and scatter over the parsley to serve.

Welsh mutton broth

Over the past few years, there have been many initiatives to promote the consumption of mutton and it is gradually making a comeback on restaurant and pub menus. It has a stronger flavour than lamb and is perfect for broths, soups and stews.

Rub the mutton joint with salt and pepper, then place in a deep cooking pot. Add enough water to cover and bring to the boil. In the meantime, roughly chop the onion, carrot and leeks. As soon as the water begins to boil, tip a cup of cold water into the pot, to encourage the froth and scum to float to the surface. Skim this off and reduce the heat to a simmer.

Continue to skim until the liquid is clear, then add the onion, carrot and half the leeks, along with the bay leaves and thyme. Simmer for about 2½–3 hours until the mutton is very tender, skimming from time to time as necessary. Leave to cool slightly, then lift out the mutton. Cut into bite-sized pieces or shred the meat finely and discard the bone.

Strain the broth into another pan and bring to a simmer. Cut the swede and turnip into 1.5cm dice and add to the broth with the pearl barley and remaining leek. Add another pinch of salt and pepper to taste and simmer for about 30–40 minutes until the vegetables and barley are tender. Return the mutton to the broth and heat for few minutes to warm through. Taste and adjust the seasoning.

Serve the soup in warm bowls, topped with a scattering of chopped parsley, with some oatcakes or rustic bread on the side.

SERVES 8

1kg mutton shoulder
  (on the bone)
sea salt and black pepper
1 large onion, peeled
1 large carrot, peeled
2 large leeks, white part
  only, trimmed
2 bay leaves
few thyme sprigs
1 large swede, about
  600g, peeled
1 large turnip, about
  600g, peeled
125g pearl barley
small handful of flat-leaf
  parsley, chopped

Hodge podge soup

SERVES 6–8

700–800g boneless shin
  of beef (or veal or
  mutton), trimmed of
  excess fat
1 large onion, peeled
1 large carrot, peeled
1 medium turnip, peeled
1 large waxy potato, such
  as Desirée or Charlotte,
  peeled
2 celery sticks, trimmed
3 tbsp olive oil
sea salt and black pepper
330ml bottle light beer
  or cider
500ml beef or veal stock
  (see page 244)
few thyme sprigs, plus
  extra leaves to garnish
1 bay leaf
20g butter, softened
20g plain flour

As the name indicates, this hearty, peasant-style soup varies according to the ingredients that happen to be in any kitchen. The British equivalent of the French *garbure*, it uses a cheap cut of meat (usually beef, mutton or veal) and whatever root vegetables are to hand. Pearl barley can be used to bulk up the soup instead of potato if you prefer.

Cut the beef into small bite-sized pieces. Chop the onion, carrot, turnip, potato and celery into even 2cm dice.

Heat a large, heavy-based saucepan and add half the olive oil. Season the beef with salt and pepper and fry in batches, for about 2 minutes on each side until evenly browned all over. Transfer the beef to a plate and set aside.

Add the remaining oil to the pan and sauté the vegetables over a medium-high heat for 4–6 minutes until lightly golden. Pour in the beer and let bubble until reduced by half. Return the beef to the pan and pour in the stock. Add the herbs and top up with enough water to cover the meat and vegetables. Bring to a gentle simmer and skim off the scum and froth that rise to the surface. Cook slowly, skimming occasionally, for 3–4 hours until the meat is meltingly tender. Discard the herbs.

Mix the butter with the flour to make a thick paste (beurre manié), then stir this into the simmering soup, a small piece at a time. Simmer, stirring, for another 5 minutes or until the soup thickens. Taste and adjust the seasoning, adding a generous grinding of pepper.

Serve the soup in warm bowls with a sprinkling of thyme leaves, as a meal in itself with plenty of crusty bread and perhaps a side salad.

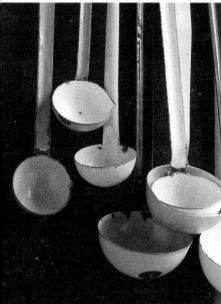

STARTERS

Mussels and bacon cooked in cider

Beetroot salad with grapefruit and goat's cheese

Prawn cocktail

Fried sprats with smoked paprika

Chicory, walnut and stilton salad

Chicken liver pâté

Salad of black pudding with poached egg

Pressed ox tongue with lamb's lettuce salad

Mussels and bacon
cooked in cider

Steaming fresh mussels in cider with sautéed bacon enhances their sweet-savoury taste to delicious effect. Much of the flavour comes from the rendered bacon fat, which melds together with the cider and mussel juices to create a tasty sauce. Serve with plenty of crusty bread to mop up the sauce.

Scrub the mussels, removing their beards and discarding any that are open and do not close when tapped. Set aside.

Heat the olive oil in a large, heavy-based pan. When hot, add the bacon and fry, turning, for 4–5 minutes until it has released most of its fat and is golden brown all over. Add the garlic and thyme and fry for another minute.

Tip in the mussels and pour in the cider. Cover with a tight-fitting lid and give the pan a gentle shake. Steam the mussels over a medium-high heat for 3–4 minutes until they have opened.

Remove the pan from the heat and grind over some black pepper. Taste the juices for seasoning; you probably won't need to add extra salt as the bacon and mussels should provide enough. Pick out and throw away any mussels that have not opened.

Sprinkle with chopped parsley and serve immediately, remembering to provide spare bowls for the discarded mussel shells.

SERVES 4

2kg live mussels
1 tbsp olive oil
150g piece of prime bacon (preferably Old Spot), cut into 3–4 pieces
5–6 garlic cloves (unpeeled), halved
few thyme sprigs
100ml dry cider
black pepper
handful of flat-leaf parsley, leaves only, chopped

Beetroot salad with
grapefruit and goat's cheese

SERVES 4

900g raw beetroot
  (roughly the same size)
rock salt
handful of thyme sprigs
1 large ruby grapefruit
few lemon thyme sprigs,
  leaves stripped
2 tbsp olive oil
2 tbsp hazelnut oil
sea salt and black pepper
pinch of caster sugar
115g goat's cheese,
  crumbled
handful of hazelnuts,
  toasted and lightly
  crushed

We love the balance of contrasting flavours and textures in this salad – sweet roasted beetroot, tangy grapefruit, creamy goat's cheese and crunchy hazelnuts. Roasting the beetroot on a layer of salt intensifies their earthy flavour.

Preheat the oven to 180°C/Gas 4. Wash the beetroot, then trim the tops and roots, and pat dry with kitchen paper. Scatter a thin layer of rock salt over a large piece of foil. Sprinkle with the thyme sprigs, then arrange the beetroot in the middle. Bring up the edges of the foil and fold them together to seal the parcel. Place on a baking tray and bake for 35–45 minutes or until the beetroot are tender when pierced with a small knife. (Larger beetroot may need an extra 15–20 minutes.)

Unwrap the parcel, transfer the beetroot to a plate and leave to cool slightly. Wearing a pair of rubber gloves (to avoid staining your hands), peel the beetroot while they are still warm, using a small knife. Cut into wedges and divide between individual serving plates.

To segment the grapefruit, slice off the top and bottom to expose the flesh. Stand on a board and cut along the curve of the fruit to remove the peel and white pith. Now, holding the fruit over a sieve set on top of a bowl, cut along the membranes to release each segment. Finally, squeeze the core to extract the juices, before discarding it.

Divide the grapefruit segments between the plates. To make the dressing, add the lemon thyme leaves to the reserved grapefruit juice and whisk in the olive and hazelnut oils. Season well with salt and pepper, adding a pinch of sugar if the dressing is too tart.

Scatter goat's cheese and hazelnuts over each serving and drizzle with the dressing. Serve immediately.

Prawn cocktail

SERVES 4

500g large raw prawns
1.5 litres court bouillon
  (see page 244)
¼ head of iceberg
  lettuce, finely shredded
few pinches of paprika

COCKTAIL SAUCE

100ml mayonnaise
  (see page 246)
2 tbsp tomato ketchup
1 tbsp brandy or cognac
1 tsp lemon juice
dash of Worcestershire
  sauce, to taste
dash of Tabasco, to taste
sea salt and white
  pepper

This was a very popular starter in the seventies and it has become fashionable again. You must, of course, use very fresh prawns. They can be poached simply in boiling salted water, but if you cook them in a court bouillon they will take on more flavour. Don't discard the stock after cooking; it can be kept in the fridge for up to a week and used to poach other seafood.

Peel the prawns, leaving the tail shells on. Make a slit along the back of each prawn and prise out the dark vein with the tip of a knife.

Pour the court bouillon into a large saucepan and bring to a simmer. Add the prawns and poach gently for 2–3 minutes until they are opaque and firm; do not overcook or they will turn rubbery. Drain and refresh in a bowl of iced water, then drain in a colander and set aside.

For the cocktail sauce, mix all the ingredients together in a bowl, seasoning with salt and white pepper to taste.

Spoon some cocktail sauce into each of four individual serving glasses. Scatter a little shredded lettuce over the sauce and arrange a few prawns on top. Repeat these layers, finishing with a small dollop of sauce. Sprinkle with a pinch of paprika and serve.

Fried sprats
with smoked paprika

Sprats, which resemble tiny herrings, do not need to be gutted or scaled. Like whitebait, you can eat them whole – they're absolutely delicious fried. Traditionally eaten with buttered brown bread and a squeeze of lemon, we prefer to serve sprats as a starter, with tartare sauce and a few salad leaves on the side.

Wash the sprats and drain, then place in a bowl. Pour on the milk and leave to soak for a few minutes. Season the flour with salt, pepper and smoked paprika. Heat the oil in a deep-fryer or other suitable deep, heavy pan to 180°C, or until a cube of bread dropped in turns golden brown in less than a minute.

Deep-fry the sprats in several batches. Lift a good handful out of the milk and toss in the seasoned flour to coat, shaking off excess. Deep-fry in the hot oil for about 2 minutes, turning once, or until golden brown and crisp. Drain on kitchen paper and sprinkle with a little more sea salt and paprika, if you wish. Keep warm in a low oven while you cook the rest.

Lightly dress the salad leaves with a little lemon juice, olive oil and seasoning, and place a neat pile on each serving plate. Divide the sprats between the plates and serve immediately, with lemon wedges and individual bowls of tartare sauce for dipping.

SERVES 6

800g fresh sprats
about 200ml milk
75g plain flour
sea salt and black pepper
2 tsp smoked paprika, plus a little extra to sprinkle if required
groundnut, rapeseed or vegetable oil, for deep-frying

TO SERVE

few handfuls of mixed salad leaves
squeeze of lemon juice
drizzle of olive oil
lemon wedges
tartare sauce (see page 119)

Chicory, walnut and stilton salad

SERVES 4

4 heads of chicory

75g stilton

60g walnuts, toasted
  and lightly crushed

DRESSING

1½ tbsp runny honey

1½ tbsp English mustard

3 tbsp walnut oil

3 tbsp olive oil

sea salt and black pepper

This delectable starter can be thrown together in a matter of minutes. Serve it on a large platter, making sure each chicory leaf is cradling some crumbled stilton, crushed walnuts and dressing – then you can dispense with the cutlery.

Trim the bases of the chicory and separate the large outer leaves. (Save the tiny leaves around the core for another salad). Arrange the leaves around one large or two smaller platters. Crumble over the stilton and scatter over the crushed walnuts, distributing them evenly among the leaves.

In a small bowl, whisk together the ingredients for the dressing, seasoning with salt and pepper to taste. Drizzle the dressing lightly over the salad. Serve immediately as a casual starter or a canapé, with a glass of white wine.

Chicken liver pâté

We call this 'poor man's pâté'. It may be inexpensive, but it makes an elegant starter and tastes divine, especially if you serve it with a red onion marmalade. Well sealed under a layer of clarified butter, this pâté keeps well for up to a week in the fridge.

De-vein the chicken livers and place in a bowl. Pour on enough milk to cover and leave to soak in the fridge for 6–8 hours. Bring to room temperature 20 minutes before preparing the pâté.

Drain and rinse the chicken livers, pat dry with kitchen paper and season well. Heat a few knobs of the butter in a pan and sauté the shallots with some seasoning over a medium heat for 5–6 minutes, until soft but not coloured. Increase the heat slightly. Add the livers and fry for 3–4 minutes until evenly browned but still pink inside. Add the brandy and flambé. When the flame dies down, add the rest of the butter to melt, then remove from the heat. Add the thyme leaves.

Immediately tip the contents of the pan into a food processor or blender and process to a smooth paste. For a very smooth texture, if required, pass through a fine sieve. Divide the pâté between four small ramekins and smooth the tops with a small spatula.

Gently melt the 175g butter in a small pan over a very low heat. Now carefully pour the golden oily layer on the surface (essentially clarified butter) into a measuring jug and discard the milky whey below. Pour or spoon some clarified butter over the top of each pâté to cover it with a thin layer. (Sealing the pâté in this way will prevent it from oxidizing and discolouring.) Sprinkle with a few thyme leaves, cover with cling film and chill for at least an hour until set.

Take the pâtés out of the fridge 15 minutes before serving. Serve them with warm toast triangles and red onion marmalade.

SERVES 4

500g chicken livers
150–200ml milk
sea salt and black pepper
75g unsalted butter, diced
2 large shallots, peeled and finely diced
generous splash of brandy
few thyme sprigs, leaves stripped

TO SEAL

175g unsalted butter
thyme leaves

TO SERVE

freshly toasted bread
red onion marmalade (see page 247)

Salad of black pudding with poached egg

SERVES 4

8–12 medium eggs
1½ tbsp cider vinegar,
  plus a dash
1 head of oak leaf lettuce
5 tbsp olive oil, plus extra
  for frying
sea salt and black pepper
450g black pudding
small handful of flat-leaf
  parsley leaves

This lovely salad can be enjoyed at any time of the year – just make sure you use good-quality black pudding. Individually made small black puddings have a much better flavour than those mass-produced ones sold in vacuum packs.

First, poach the eggs; it is preferable to do this in batches, poaching no more than 3 eggs at a time. Bring a pan of water to a simmer. Add a dash of vinegar and swirl the water with a spoon to create a whirlpool effect in the middle. One at a time, crack the eggs into a small bowl or ramekin and gently slide them into the whirlpool. Poach for 3 minutes until the whites are set but the yolks are still runny in the centre. Lift the eggs out with a slotted spoon into a bowl of iced water to stop further cooking. Set aside while you poach the rest.

Wash and separate the lettuce leaves. Tear the larger ones into smaller pieces and divide them between serving plates. For the dressing, whisk together the cider vinegar, olive oil and some seasoning.

Cut the black pudding into 4 portions, then cut each piece lengthways in half. Heat a wide frying pan until hot. Pour in a thin layer of olive oil, then add the black pudding. Fry for 3–4 minutes on each side until nicely browned and crisp around the edges. Reheat the eggs in a pan of simmering water for about a minute.

Carefully crumble the black pudding over the lettuce leaves and scatter over the parsley. Using a slotted spoon, lift out the eggs, drain them well and pat the bases dry with kitchen paper. Arrange two or three on top of each salad. Drizzle over the dressing and grind over some black pepper. Serve at once.

Pressed ox tongue
with lamb's lettuce salad

Ox tongue makes a delicious cold starter. You may need to order one in advance from your butcher – remember that you'll need to soak it overnight before cooking. Refrigerate any leftover tongue and use as a sandwich filler.

Drain and rinse the tongue, then put it into a large cooking pot with the vegetables. Pour in enough cold water to cover, bring to a simmer and skim off the scum from the surface until the water is clear. Add the bouquet garni, peppercorns, juniper berries and a pinch of salt. Simmer over a gentle heat for 3½–4 hours, topping up with boiling water as necessary to keep the tongue covered. When cooked, the skin should peel away easily from the flesh. To test, pierce with a small knife; the meat should feel tender. Lift the tongue out of the poaching stock and leave to cool slightly. Reserve the liquor.

Line a small loaf tin or cylindrical mould, about 450g capacity, with cling film, leaving enough overhanging the sides to fold over the top. While still warm, peel off the coarse skin from the tongue with a small knife, or scrape it off with a spoon if you find this easier. Pack the tongue into the prepared tin, trimming to fit as necessary. Spoon over a little poaching liquid to fill any gaps as you pack the mould. Finally, pour enough liquor over the tongue to cover it in a thin layer. Fold over the excess cling film to seal and put a couple of heavy tins on top to weigh the tongue down. Chill for a few hours or overnight until set.

Take the tongue out of the fridge 20–30 minutes before serving. Place the salad leaves in a bowl. For the dressing, whisk the vinegar and olive oil together in a bowl with some salt and pepper. Just before serving, drizzle the dressing over the salad leaves and toss lightly.

Unmould the pressed tongue and cut into slices. Arrange 3 or 4 slices on each plate with the salad leaves and a few caper berries alongside.

SERVES 4

1 unsalted ox tongue, about 1.2kg, soaked overnight in plenty of cold water
1 large onion, peeled and halved
1 celery stick, peeled and cut into 3 pieces
1 large carrot, peeled and cut into 3 pieces
1 large leek, trimmed and cut into 3 pieces
1 bouquet garni (1 bay leaf, few each thyme and parsley sprigs, tied together)
1 tsp black peppercorns
1 tsp juniper berries
sea salt

SALAD

100g mixed lamb's lettuce and frisée leaves
2 tsp cider vinegar (or white wine vinegar)
3 tbsp olive oil

TO SERVE

few handfuls of caper berries

CATCH OF THE DAY

Hake in beer batter with mushy peas

Dover sole with brown butter and grapes

Crab cakes with mayonnaise

Seafood salad

Salmon steaks with brown shrimps, capers and parsley

Cod with clams and smoked bacon

Grilled kippers

Baked stuffed herrings

Baked bream fillets with fennel
  and orange

Rainbow trout with sorrel and capers

Stewed eel

Grilled lemon sole with tartare sauce

Somerset fish casserole

Hake in beer batter
with mushy peas

Along with savoury pies, fish 'n' chips with mushy peas represents true British pub food. Fry the chips first and keep warm in a low oven – uncovered to keep them crisp.

Check the hake fillets for pin-bones, removing any that you come across with kitchen tweezers. Chill until ready to cook.

To make the batter, sift the flour, rice flour, baking powder and a generous pinch each of salt and pepper into a large bowl and make a well in the centre. In a smaller bowl, stir together the ale, vodka and honey, then pour into the well and whisk until the mixture is well combined. Cover and let the batter stand for an hour before using.

For the mushy peas, drop the mint leaves into a pan one-third filled with salted water and bring to the boil. Add the peas and blanch for 2–3 minutes until tender. Drain, reserving the water. Tip the peas into a food processor and add the wine vinegar and some seasoning. Pulse to a rough purée, adding a little of the reserved liquid as necessary to get the desired texture. Check the seasoning and keep warm.

Heat the oil in a deep-fryer or other suitable heavy pan to 200°C, or until a little of the batter dropped in bubbles vigorously and browns in 30 seconds. Deep-fry the fish fillets two at a time. Coat with a little flour, then dip into the batter, letting any excess drip off, and gently lower into the hot oil. Deep-fry for 4–6 minutes until golden all over, turning the fillets over halfway. Remove with a slotted spoon and drain on kitchen paper. Make sure that the oil returns to 200°C before you deep-fry the other fillets. Keep the fried fish warm in a low oven while you fry the other batch and reheat the mushy peas if necessary.

Serve the fish as soon as they are all cooked, with the mushy peas, chips and tartare sauce.

SERVES 4

4 hake fillets, or other chunky firm-textured white fish fillets, about 140g each
50g plain flour, plus extra to coat
50g rice flour
2 tsp baking powder
sea salt and black pepper
150ml light ale
40ml vodka
½ tsp runny honey
groundnut or vegetable oil, for deep-frying

MUSHY PEAS

few mint sprigs, leaves only
350g frozen peas
1 tbsp white wine vinegar

TO SERVE

chips (see page 184)
tartare sauce (see page 119)

Dover sole with brown butter and grapes

SERVES 4

2–3 tbsp plain flour
sea salt and black pepper
2 Dover sole, about
  350–450g each, skinned
  and filleted
2 tbsp olive oil
200g unsalted butter,
  diced
juice of 1 lemon
50g flaked almonds,
  toasted
20–25 seedless green
  grapes, skinned and
  halved

This dish is our take on classic *sole veronique* – sole fillets poached in a creamy sauce, then grilled and garnished with grapes. Our version pairs the fish with a nutty brown butter, which is the perfect foil for the sweet grapes. If Dover sole seems extravagant, use a less costly member of the sole family – lemon sole, perhaps. To make it easier to skin the grapes, first blanch them in boiling water for a minute, then refresh under cold running water.

Preheat the oven to low. Tip the flour onto a plate and season with salt and pepper. Coat the fish fillets in the seasoned flour, shaking off any excess.

Cook the sole fillets in 2 batches. Heat a large frying pan, then add half the olive oil with a knob of the butter. Fry the fish for 3–4 minutes until golden brown and just firm. Remove to a warm platter and cover with foil while you fry the rest of the fish, using the rest of the oil and another knob of the butter. When the fillets are all cooked, place the tray in the low oven to keep warm.

Return the frying pan to the heat and add the rest of the butter to melt. Cook over a medium heat until the melted butter turns to a light nut brown colour. Immediately take the pan off the heat and pour in the lemon juice. Carefully pour the butter into another small pan and discard the milk solids. Gently reheat the brown butter as necessary, then tip in the flaked almonds and grapes. Season well to taste.

Place two sole fillets on each warm serving plate and spoon over the sauce, making sure that the grapes and almonds are distributed evenly. Serve at once, with sautéed potatoes and French beans.

Crab cakes with mayonnaise

You can use a mixture of white and brown meat for these crab cakes – just try to ensure that you end up with at least as much crabmeat as mashed potato. Serve with a mixed salad for a delectable starter, light lunch or supper.

Cut the potatoes into even-sized chunks and cook in boiling salted water for 15–20 minutes, until soft. Drain and while still hot, press through a potato ricer into a large bowl, or mash well until smooth. Beat in the butter and a generous pinch each of salt and pepper.

Heat the olive oil in a small pan, then add the shallot with some seasoning and sweat over a medium heat for 6–8 minutes, stirring occasionally, until soft and translucent.

Beat the shallot into the mashed potato, then fold through the mayonnaise, lemon zest and juice, and chopped herbs. Season well. Pick through the crabmeat discarding any stray pieces of shell, then stir through the potato mixture. Cover and chill for 30 minutes.

Divide the mixture into 6 even portions and shape into patties. If you wish, use a 7–8cm pastry ring to neaten the shape. Season the flour with salt and pepper. Lightly coat each patty with seasoned flour, then dip in the beaten egg and finally into the breadcrumbs to coat all over. Arrange them on a tray lined with non-stick baking paper and chill for 30 minutes to set the shape, if you have time.

Preheat the oven to 200°C/Gas 6 and put a baking sheet in to heat up. Heat a thin layer of groundnut oil in a large frying pan and fry the crab cakes lightly for 2–3 minutes on each side until golden brown. Transfer to the baking sheet and finish cooking in the oven for 8–10 minutes.

Place a crab cake on each serving plate and arrange a pile of salad and herb leaves alongside. Add a dollop of mayonnaise and serve at once.

SERVES 6

500g potatoes, peeled
20g butter
sea salt and black pepper
1½ tbsp olive oil
1 large shallot, peeled and finely chopped
2–3 tbsp mayonnaise (see page 246)
finely grated zest of 1 lemon
1 tbsp lemon juice
handful of mixed herb sprigs, such as chervil, basil and parsley, chopped
500g white crabmeat
25g plain flour
2 medium eggs, lightly beaten
100g fine white breadcrumbs (made from one- or two-day old bread)
groundnut oil, for frying

TO SERVE

few handfuls of mixed salad and herb leaves
mayonnaise (see page 246)

Seafood salad

SERVES 4–6

1.5 litres court bouillon
   (see page 244)
sea salt and black pepper
400g baby octopus,
   cleaned
400g baby squid,
   cleaned
400g large raw prawns
1 small live lobster, about
   650–700g
8 live razor clams,
   scrubbed clean
500g live mussels,
   scrubbed clean

DRESSING

finely grated zest of
   2 lemons
finely grated zest of
   1 lime
juice of 1 lemon
4–5 tbsp extra virgin
   olive oil
small handful of dill,
   leaves only, chopped

Moving on from the days when pickled seafood was typical pub fare, we offer customers a zesty seafood salad. Use crab claws in place of lobster if you like, or introduce other seafood. Serve as a light lunch, with crusty bread.

Bring the court bouillon to a simmer in a large saucepan (that will take the lobster). Add a pinch of salt and pepper, then poach the baby octopus and squid for 3 minutes until opaque and just cooked through but still tender. Transfer to a bowl, using a slotted spoon. Add the prawns to the stock and poach for 2–3 minutes until just opaque and firm. Lift out with the slotted spoon and leave to cool on a plate. Finally, put the lobster into the stock, cover the pan with a lid and poach for 7–8 minutes. Remove and leave to cool for a few minutes.

Heat another large saucepan until hot. Tip in the razor clams and add a splash of water. Cover with a tight-fitting lid and steam for a minute. Add the mussels, put the lid back on and give the pan a shake. Steam for 3 minutes until the clams and mussels have opened; discard any that stay closed. Transfer the shellfish to another bowl; leave to cool.

Meanwhile, remove the flesh from the lobster tails. First pull apart the claws from the body. Crack the tough claw shells with the back of a cleaver (or a nutcracker) and set aside. Pull the head away from the tail. Cut through the bottom shell of the tail with a pair of scissors to remove the meat. Cut into bite-sized pieces and place in a large bowl.

Remove the flesh from the razor clam shells and chop into bite-sized pieces. Shell the mussels and add to the lobster with the clams. Chop the squid and octopus into bite-sized pieces and add to the bowl.

For the dressing, whisk the ingredients together and season well with salt and pepper. Saving a little, toss the dressing with the seafood until well mixed. Transfer to a serving platter then arrange the prawns and lobster claws on top. Drizzle over the reserved dressing and serve.

Salmon steaks with
brown shrimps, capers and parsley

SERVES 4

4 thick salmon steaks on
  the bone, about
  180–200g each
sea salt and black pepper
2 tbsp olive oil
50g butter
200g Morecambe Bay or
  brown shrimps, peeled
80g capers, rinsed and
  drained
juice of 1 lemon
bunch of flat-leaf
  parsley, leaves only,
  chopped

Here robust salmon steaks are paired with the punchy and gutsy flavours of capers and brown shrimp. Accompany with sautéed potatoes and steamed green beans or a watercress salad for a satisfying main course.

Season the salmon steaks on both sides with salt and pepper. Place a large frying pan over a medium-high heat. When hot, add the olive oil to the pan, followed by the salmon fillets. Fry for about 2–2½ minutes on each side until golden brown but still pink in the middle; they should feel slightly springy when pressed. Remove to a warm plate and set aside to rest.

Add the butter to the pan and, as it melts, tip in the brown shrimps and capers. Toss over a medium heat for 1–2 minutes. Add the lemon juice and chopped parsley and toss to combine. Season generously with pepper; you probably won't need any more salt.

Spoon the shrimp and caper mixture onto warm serving plates and lay the salmon steaks on top. Serve immediately.

Cod with clams and smoked bacon

The delicate flavour of cod is hard to beat, but sadly our native cod have been in decline for a while, due to overfishing. For a clear conscience, be sure to ask your fishmonger for farmed cod or line-caught Pacific cod.

Remove any pin-bones from the cod fillets with kitchen tweezers, then season well. Scrub the clams and rinse well in several changes of water to clean out any grit that may be trapped inside their shells. Discard any that are open and do not close when tapped. Set aside.

Heat a large frying pan and add half the olive oil. When hot, lay the fish fillets in the pan, skin side down, along with a couple of thyme sprigs. Fry for about 2–3 minutes until the skin is crisp, then carefully turn the fish and add a few knobs of butter to the pan. Baste the fish fillets with the melted butter as they cook for another 30 seconds. Remove to a plate and set aside.

Heat the remaining oil in a large saucepan (one with a tight-fitting lid). Add the bacon, with a few thyme sprigs, and sauté for a few minutes until it turns lightly golden and releases its fat. Pour in the wine and bring to the boil. Tip the clams into the pan, cover the pan tightly and increase the heat to high. Steam the clams, shaking the pan gently a few times, for 3–4 minutes until the shells open.

Remove the lid and discard any unopened clams. Taste the cooking juices and adjust the seasoning as necessary. You probably won't need to add salt, as the clams and bacon should provide sufficient. Add the fish fillets to the pan to warm through for a minute.

Divide the cod, clams and pan juices between warm, shallow bowls. Garnish with thyme and serve, with crusty bread or chips on the side.

SERVES 4

4 thick cod fillets, about 200g each
sea salt and black pepper
1kg live clams
3 tbsp olive oil
small handful of thyme sprigs, plus extra to garnish
few knobs of butter
200g smoked streaky bacon, roughly chopped
250ml dry white wine

Grilled kippers

SERVES 4
4 kippers, about
  200g each
50g unsalted butter,
  softened
1 heaped tsp English
  mustard

GRILLED TOMATOES
4 large vine tomatoes,
  halved
sea salt and black pepper
olive oil, to drizzle

TO SERVE
flat-leaf parsley
lemon wedges
brown bread, sliced and
  buttered

It's time to revive the popularity of kippers – they are quick and easy to cook for breakfast and taste absolutely delicious. They also make a great brunch or lunch, served with brown bread and grilled tomatoes.

Preheat the grill to its highest setting. First cook the tomatoes. Place, cut side up, on a lightly oiled baking tray. Season with salt and pepper and drizzle over a little olive oil. Grill for about 8–10 minutes until the tomatoes are beginning to soften but still holding their shape.

Meanwhile, line two large baking trays with foil and butter lightly. Lay the kippers skin side down on the trays. Mix the remaining butter with the mustard and some black pepper. Spread over the kippers.

When the tomatoes are ready, transfer them to a low oven to keep warm. Place the kippers under the grill for 3–4 minutes until just cooked through; they should feel just firm when lightly pressed. Transfer to warm plates and garnish with parsley and lemon wedges. Serve immediately, with the grilled tomatoes and brown bread.

Baked stuffed herrings

SERVES 4

4 small herrings, about 175–200g each, cleaned and gutted

sea salt and black pepper

8 tsp Dijon or English mustard

7–8 tbsp medium oatmeal

olive oil, to drizzle

STUFFING

2 tbsp olive oil

2 rashers smoked bacon, chopped

1 medium onion, peeled and chopped

150g chestnut mushrooms, trimmed and roughly chopped

2 tbsp medium oatmeal

1 tbsp lemon juice

small bunch of flat-leaf parsley, leaves only, chopped

few lemon thyme sprigs, leaves stripped

TO SERVE

lemon wedges

crusty bread

Stuffing herrings with a breadcrumb or oatmeal mixture was originally a way to bulk up the meal and make the fish go further. In any case, it is a delicious way to treat this rich, oily fish. Our mushroom, bacon and oatmeal stuffing has a great flavour and texture; it can also be used to stuff chicken or pork.

Preheat the oven to 200°C/Gas 6. To prepare the stuffing, heat the olive oil in a frying pan over a medium heat. Add the bacon and fry for 3–5 minutes until browned and most of the fat has rendered. Add the onion, mushrooms and some seasoning. Cook, stirring occasionally, for another 4–6 minutes until the onion is soft. Take the pan off the heat and stir in the oatmeal, lemon juice and herbs. Transfer to a bowl, then taste and adjust the seasoning. Leave to cool slightly.

Rub the herrings all over with salt and pepper, seasoning the cavities as well. Brush or rub each side of the fish with mustard, then coat with oatmeal. Place on a lightly oiled baking tray and spoon the mushroom and bacon stuffing into the cavities.

Drizzle the herrings with olive oil and bake for 15–20 minutes, carefully turning each fish halfway through cooking. The herrings are ready when they feel just firm if lightly pressed, and the flesh comes away from the bone easily.

Serve the stuffed herrings immediately, with some lemon wedges and crusty bread on the side.

Baked bream fillets
with fennel and orange

This is a healthy and refreshing way to serve bream fillets. If you can't get hold of bream, then sea bass fillets would work just as well. Serve with new potatoes.

Preheat the oven to 200°C/Gas 6. Trim the bream fillets to neaten, and remove any pin-bones with kitchen tweezers. Score the skin of each fillet at 5mm intervals. Chill until ready to cook.

Halve each fennel bulb and slice finely, using a mandoline if possible. Scatter the fennel over the base of two lightly oiled, deep baking trays.

To segment the oranges, slice off the top and bottom to just expose the flesh. Stand on a board and cut along the curve of the fruit to remove the peel and white pith. Now, holding the fruit over a sieve set on top of a bowl, cut along the membranes to release each segment. Finally, squeeze the core to extract the juices before discarding.

Scatter the orange segments over the fennel. Trickle over the reserved orange juice, then add the wine. Sprinkle with the sugar and some salt and pepper. Cover each tray with foil and place in the oven. Bake for 10–15 minutes until the fennel is just tender.

Remove the foil and scatter the basil leaves over the oranges and fennel. Rub the bream fillets with a little olive oil and season well with salt and pepper. Lay them on top of the oranges and fennel. Drizzle over a little more olive oil and sprinkle with more salt and pepper. Scatter over the thyme sprigs.

Bake for 8–10 minutes until the fish is opaque and feels slightly firm when pressed. Divide the fennel and orange between warm plates and top with the fish fillets. Serve at once.

SERVES 4

4 bream fillets, with skin, about 150g each
2 medium fennel bulbs, trimmed (fronds reserved if intact)
2 large oranges
75–100ml dry white wine
2 tsp caster sugar
sea salt and black pepper
few basil sprigs, leaves only
olive oil, to rub and drizzle
small handful of thyme sprigs

Rainbow trout with sorrel and capers

SERVES 4

4 small rainbow trout,
  about 300–320g each,
  scaled and gutted
sea salt and black pepper
handful of thyme sprigs
8 knobs of butter
splash of dry white wine

SAUCE

1 small shallot, peeled
  and finely chopped
3 tbsp white wine or
  cider vinegar
3 tbsp water
200g unsalted butter,
  chilled and diced
about 20 caper berries,
  rinsed
small bunch of sorrel
  leaves, finely shredded

TO SERVE

lemon wedges

The citrusy tang of fresh sorrel is an ideal match for oily fish like rainbow trout. To retain the sprightly flavour and vibrant colour of the leaves, add them to the buttery sauce at the last moment, just as you are about to serve.

Preheat the oven to 180°C/Gas 4. Pat the trout dry with kitchen paper and score the skin several times on one side, on the diagonal. Rub the fish all over with salt and pepper, including the cavity.

Lay the trout in one large or two smaller oiled baking trays. Stuff a few thyme sprigs into each cavity, then dot a couple of knobs of butter on top of each fish. Pour a splash of wine into the tray and sprinkle a little more salt and pepper over the fish. Bake for 15–20 minutes until the fish is opaque and just firm; the flesh will come away from the bone easily when it is ready.

While the fish is cooking, make the sauce. Put the shallot, vinegar and water into a small saucepan, bring to the boil and let bubble until reduced by two-thirds, to about 2 tbsp. Turn the heat down to low and gradually whisk in the butter, a knob at a time. The finished sauce should be pale and creamy, and have the consistency of single cream. Stir in the caper berries and season with pepper, and a little salt to taste if required.

Transfer the cooked fish to warm plates. Add the sorrel to the warm sauce and immediately spoon over each trout. Serve at once, with lemon wedges.

Stewed eel

SERVES 4

700g skinned, filleted eel
(about 1kg unprepared
weight)
30g plain flour
sea salt and black pepper
1½ tbsp olive oil
1 large onion, peeled and
thinly sliced
generous splash of dry
white wine
500ml chicken stock (see
page 243) or fish stock
(see page 245)
1 bay leaf
few thyme sprigs
finely pared zest of
1 lemon
1 tbsp lemon juice
pinch of saffron strands
2–3 tbsp double cream
few flat-leaf parsley
sprigs, leaves only,
chopped

Freshwater eels were once abundant in the Thames estuary. Nowadays, you are rather more likely to get a large seawater eel from your fishmonger, and you'll need to order it in advance. Eels are sold live, as their oily flesh degrades quickly, and they are tricky to handle. To save the hassle, get your fishmonger to prepare it for you.

Cut the eel into 5cm pieces. Season the flour with salt and pepper, then use to lightly coat the eel pieces, saving any excess. Heat the olive oil in a wide pan and fry the eel in batches for 4–5 minutes until evenly browned all over. Drain on kitchen paper. When all the eel pieces are browned, tip away the excess oil from the pan, leaving behind 2 tbsp. Add the onion to the pan with some seasoning and sweat over a medium-low heat for 10 minutes or until soft and translucent.

Tip in any remaining seasoned flour and stir for a minute or two. Add the wine and let it bubble until the pan is quite dry. Pour in the stock and add the herbs, lemon zest, lemon juice and saffron. Stir and simmer for a minute. Return the eel pieces to the pan, cover and simmer gently for about 20–30 minutes until the eel is tender.

Stir in the cream and adjust the seasoning with salt and pepper. Sprinkle over some chopped parsley and serve warm. As you are eating eel, you will need to keep an eye out for small bones.

Grilled lemon sole
with tartare sauce

It is far easier to grill rather than pan-fry a whole fish, particularly a delicate-fleshed fish like lemon sole. Serve with oven-baked chips or new potatoes and green beans or courgettes for a satisfying main dish.

First prepare the tartare sauce. Put all of the ingredients into a bowl and stir to combine, then taste and adjust the seasoning. Set aside.

Preheat the grill to high. Rinse the lemon soles and pat thoroughly dry with kitchen paper. Score the skin in two or three places on each side with a sharp knife. Rub both sides with a little olive oil and a few pinches each of salt and pepper.

Lay the fish on one large or two smaller oiled baking sheets and drizzle over a little more olive oil. Grill the fish for 4–5 minutes on each side until just cooked through.

Carefully transfer the fish to warm oval plates. Serve with the lemon wedges and tartare sauce on the side.

SERVES 4

4 small lemon soles,
  about 300–350g each,
  gutted and trimmed
olive oil, to rub and
  drizzle
sea salt and black pepper

TARTARE SAUCE

200ml mayonnaise
  (see page 246)
1 large cornichon, finely
  diced
1 shallot, peeled and
  finely diced
1½–2 tsp capers, rinsed
  and chopped
1–2 tsp lemon juice,
  to taste
small bunch of flat-leaf
  parsley, chopped

TO SERVE

lemon wedges

Somerset fish casserole

SERVES 4

500g firm white fish
  fillets, such as coley or
  brill
20g plain flour
sea salt and black pepper
40g butter, diced
2 onions, peeled and
  thinly sliced
2 anchovy fillets in oil,
  finely crushed
200ml medium dry cider
200ml chicken stock (see
  page 243) or fish stock
  (see page 245)
100ml double cream
squeeze of lemon juice
2 apples, such as
  Braeburn or Cox
few flat-leaf parsley
  sprigs, leaves only,
  finely chopped
  (optional)

In Somerset, where apples are abundant, fish is commonly cooked with cider, akin to the way it is cooked with white wine in the wine-producing areas of Europe. Taking the concept a step further, this dish is served topped with fried apple slices, adding an element of sweetness.

Cut the fish into bite-sized chunks, removing any pin-bones with tweezers. Put the flour into a shallow dish and season with a little salt and pepper. Toss the fish pieces in the flour to coat, saving any excess.

Melt a few knobs of the butter in a wide heavy-based pan and fry the fish in batches for 1½–2 minutes on each side until evenly golden all over. As each batch is cooked, transfer to a plate, using a slotted spoon. Set the fish aside.

Add a little more butter to the pan and cook the onions for 8–10 minutes, stirring occasionally, until soft. Tip in any remaining seasoned flour, along with the anchovies. Fry, stirring, for a minute or two, then pour in the cider. Let bubble for a few minutes to cook off the alcohol and reduce the liquid. Pour in the stock and cream and simmer for a further 5–10 minutes until thickened to a light coating consistency. Season well to taste with salt, pepper and a squeeze of lemon juice.

Peel and core the apples, then slice thinly into rings. Melt a few knobs of butter in a wide frying pan and fry the apple rings for a few minutes on each side until golden. Set aside.

Return the fish pieces to their pan and turn to coat in the sauce. Simmer gently for a few minutes until the fish is just firm and cooked through. Transfer to a warm serving dish and arrange the fried apple slices on top. Sprinkle with chopped parsley, if you wish, and serve.

Pies and Savoury Tarts

Asparagus and spring onion tart

Smoked salmon and watercress tart

Beef cobbler

Cottage pie with Guinness

Huntingdon fidget pie

Chicken and smoked bacon pie

Cornish pasties

Steak and kidney pie

Bosworth goat's cheese tart

Montgomery cheddar and potato pie

Tomato, goat's cheese and herb tart

Asparagus and spring onion tart

SERVES 6

300g shortcrust pastry
  (see page 248)
1 medium egg white,
  lightly beaten, to glaze
10 spring onions,
  trimmed
20g butter
sea salt and black pepper
350g asparagus spears,
  trimmed and lower
  part of stalks peeled
2 large eggs, plus 2 large
  yolks
250ml double cream
100g medium cheddar,
  grated

Bake this delectable tart when homegrown asparagus is available in May and early June, as a celebration of spring.

Roll out the pastry on a lightly floured surface to a large round, the thickness of a £1 coin. Use to line a 23–24cm round tart tin, 2–3cm deep, with removable base, leaving a little excess overhanging the rim. Chill for at least 30 minutes.

Preheat the oven to 200°C/Gas 6. Line the tart case with baking paper and dried or ceramic baking beans and bake 'blind' for 15–20 minutes. Remove the paper and beans and bake for a further 5 minutes. Leave to cool slightly, then trim off the excess pastry around the rim. Brush the inside of the pastry case with egg white to glaze. Leave to cool while you prepare the filling. Reduce the oven setting to 180°C/Gas 4.

Slice the spring onions on the diagonal. Melt the butter in a pan, add the spring onions with a little seasoning and sauté over a medium heat until soft but not browned. Remove and allow to cool slightly. Add the asparagus spears to a pan of boiling salted water and blanch for 2–3 minutes; they should still retain a bite. Drain and refresh under cold running water; drain well. Halve the asparagus spears lengthways.

Whisk the eggs, egg yolks and cream together in a bowl. Add three-quarters of the cheese and season well with salt and pepper.

Sprinkle half the remaining cheese over the pastry base, then scatter over a layer of spring onions. Arrange the asparagus spears on top, then carefully pour on the creamy mix until it reaches to just below the rim of the pastry. Sprinkle with the remaining cheese and bake for 35–45 minutes until the filling is set and golden. Leave to cool in the tin slightly before unmoulding. Serve warm or at room temperature.

Smoked salmon and watercress tart

SERVES 6

300g shortcrust pastry
  (see page 248)
1 medium egg white,
  lightly beaten, to glaze
50g watercress
120g smoked salmon
3 large eggs
400ml crème fraîche
finely grated zest of
  1½ lemons
2 tsp lemon juice
sea salt and black pepper

Smoked salmon and watercress are ideal partners and they come together perfectly in the creamy custard filling for this delicious tart. Serve as a summery starter, or as a light lunch with a leafy salad and crusty bread.

Roll out the pastry on a lightly floured surface to a large round, the thickness of a £1 coin. Use to line a 23–24cm tart tin, 2.5cm deep, with removable base, leaving a little excess pastry overhanging the rim. Chill the pastry case for at least 30 minutes to allow it to rest and firm up.

Preheat the oven to 200°C/Gas 6. Line the pastry with baking paper and dried beans or ceramic baking beans and bake 'blind' for about 15–20 minutes. Remove the paper and beans and return to the oven for another 5–10 minutes until the base is cooked. Leave to cool for a few minutes, then cut off the excess pastry around the rim with a sharp knife, so the pastry edge is level with the rim of the tin. While still warm, brush the inside of the pastry case with egg white. Turn the oven setting down to 180°C/Gas 4.

Pick the watercress leaves, discarding the woody stalks. Spread the leaves evenly over the base of the pastry case. Roughly tear the smoked salmon into small pieces and scatter over the watercress.

Lightly beat the eggs, crème fraîche, lemon zest and juice together in a bowl and season well with salt and pepper. Carefully pour this mixture over the salmon and watercress and grind a little more black pepper over the top. Bake for 35–45 minutes until the filling is set and golden on top.

Leave to cool in the tin for 5–10 minutes before unmoulding. Slice and serve with a watercress and rocket salad on the side, if you wish.

Beef cobbler

This rich beef stew with its cheesy scone topping is a lovely alternative to a steak pie with a pastry lid. As the scones cook on top of the stew, they absorb some of the sauce from below, but remain light and fluffy on top. Just make sure you are ready to serve the cobbler as soon as the scones are cooked, otherwise they'll go soggy if left on the warm stew for a while. If you want to prepare the cobbler ahead, bake the scones separately – they'll take about 10–12 minutes at 220°C/Gas 7. Arrange them on top of the stew to warm through and serve.

Preheat the oven to 150°C/Gas 2. Cut the beef steak into bite-sized chunks and mix the flour with a little salt and pepper. Lightly coat the meat with the seasoned flour, saving any excess. Place a flameproof casserole dish over a medium heat and add a little olive oil. When hot, brown the meat in batches, for 2–3 minutes on each side. Transfer the browned beef to a plate and add more oil as needed between batches.

Add a little more oil to the casserole and fry the onions, garlic and bacon over a high heat for 6–8 minutes until golden brown. Tip in any remaining seasoned flour and stir well. Pour in the wine and let it boil until reduced by a third. In the meantime, cut the carrots and parsnips into large chunks, and cut the leeks and celery into 4cm slices. Add these to the casserole and pour in the stock. Return the beef and add the herbs with some salt and pepper.

Bring to a low simmer, then put the lid on and transfer the casserole to the oven. Cook for about 2–2¼ hours until the meat is tender, stirring halfway through cooking. Skim off any fat from the surface of the liquor. If the sauce is a little too thin, strain the liquor into a pan and boil until reduced and thickened. Taste and adjust the seasoning, then pour the liquor back over the meat and vegetables. Keep warm.

Increase the oven setting to 200°C/ Gas 6. To make the scone topping, sift the flour and salt together into a large bowl. Rub in the butter with your fingers until the mixture resembles fine breadcrumbs, then stir through all but 2 tbsp of the cheese. Make a well in the centre, pour in most of the milk and mix lightly to a dough, adding more milk to mix if necessary. Turn onto a lightly floured surface and knead gently until just smooth. Press the dough out to a 1.5–2cm thickness and stamp out rounds, using a 6–7cm pastry cutter.

Brush the dough rounds lightly with milk and arrange on top of the stew, leaving a little space in between to allow for expansion. Sprinkle them with the reserved cheese. Bake for 20 minutes, or until well risen and golden brown. Leave to stand for 5 minutes before serving.

SERVES 4–6

900g braising beef steak
3 tbsp plain flour
sea salt and black pepper
2–3 tbsp olive oil
2 onions, peeled and
  chopped
1 garlic clove, peeled and
  finely crushed
4 smoked bacon rashers,
  derinded and chopped
600ml red wine
2 carrots, peeled
2 parsnips, peeled
2 leeks, trimmed
2 celery sticks, trimmed
600ml beef stock
  (see page 244)
2 bay leaves
few thyme sprigs

SCONE TOPPING

250g self-raising flour,
  plus extra for kneading
½ tsp fine sea salt
50g butter, diced
150g medium cheddar,
  grated
about 150ml whole milk,
  plus extra to glaze

Cottage pie with Guinness

SERVES 6–7

2 tbsp olive oil
900g lean minced beef
sea salt and black pepper
3 medium onions, peeled
  and finely chopped
2 garlic cloves, peeled
  and finely chopped
few thyme sprigs,
  leaves only
2 plum tomatoes,
  chopped
2 tbsp tomato purée
330ml bottle Guinness
5 tbsp Worcestershire
  sauce
300ml chicken stock
  (see page 243)
1kg floury potatoes, such
  as Maris Piper or King
  Edward, peeled and
  roughly cubed
50g butter
2 tbsp finely grated
  parmesan or cheddar,
  plus extra for grating
1 large egg yolk

A deeply savoury cottage pie makes a comforting mid-week supper, particularly when it's cold and dreary outside. You might like to add some diced carrots to the pie base for extra colour, or serve some glazed baby carrots on the side.

Place a large frying pan over a high heat and add a thin layer of olive oil. Season the mince with salt and pepper and fry, stirring, in two or three batches, until nicely browned. Once cooked, tip the mince into a sieve or colander to drain off the fat.

Place another large pan over a medium-high heat and add a little olive oil. When hot, fry the onions, with the garlic and thyme, for 8–10 minutes until soft and golden. Add the browned mince, tomatoes and tomato purée. Stir constantly for 4–5 minutes.

Add the Guinness and Worcestershire sauce and boil until the liquid has reduced by half. Pour in the stock and return to the boil. Turn the heat down and simmer for 20–25 minutes, by which time the mixture should be thick and glossy. Continue to simmer for another 5–10 minutes if it doesn't seem quite thick enough. Remove from the heat.

Preheat the oven to 180°C/Gas 4. Meanwhile, add the potatoes to a pan of salted water, bring to the boil and cook until tender. Drain and return to the hot pan for 15 seconds or so, to dry out, then take off the heat. Pass the potatoes through a potato ricer back into the pan or mash smoothly. Mix through the butter, cheese and egg yolk. Taste and adjust the seasoning.

Spoon the mince mixture into the bottom of a 2 litre pie dish. Spoon the mashed potato on top and rough up the surface with a fork. Grate over some extra cheese and bake in the oven for about 30 minutes until bubbling and golden brown.

Huntingdon fidget pie

This tasty, satisfying pie was invented a long time ago – most probably to keep the workers sustained during busy apple harvests. The simple filling consists of bacon, onion, apples and cider, with a handful of parsley thrown in for good measure. It takes little effort to make.

Preheat the oven to 190°C/Gas 5. Peel, core and roughly chop the apples into bite-sized chunks, then place in a large bowl. Cut the bacon into 3cm squares and add to the apples with the onion and parsley. Toss to mix, adding a pinch of sugar if the apples are very tart, and seasoning well with salt and pepper. Transfer the filling to a 20cm round pie dish.

In a bowl, blend the flour with a little of the cider to make a paste, then gradually stir in the rest of the cider, keeping the mixture smooth. Pour over the filling in the pie dish; there should be enough to almost cover it.

Roll out the pastry to a large round, the thickness of a £1 coin, and cut out a circle for the pie lid, slightly larger all round than the dish. Cut 2cm wide strips from the pastry trimmings to go around the rim of the pie dish.

Brush the edge of the pie dish with water and position the pastry strips on the rim, joining them to fit as necessary. Press down lightly all the way round. Brush the strip with water, then lift the pastry lid on top of the pie and press the edges together to seal. Crimp the edges.

With a sharp knife, cut a cross in the centre of the pastry lid, then fold the points back a little to reveal the filling. Brush the pastry with beaten egg yolk. Put the pie on a baking tray and bake for about 50–60 minutes until the pastry is golden and the filling is cooked.

SERVES 4–6

300g shortcrust pastry
  (see page 248)
2 medium Bramley
  apples
450g piece of unsmoked
  back bacon, derinded
1 large onion, peeled and
  roughly chopped
handful of flat-leaf
  parsley, leaves only,
  chopped
pinch of caster sugar
  (optional)
sea salt and black pepper
2 tbsp plain flour
300ml medium dry cider
1 egg yolk, beaten,
  to glaze

Chicken and smoked bacon pie

SERVES 4–6

1 organic or free-range
  chicken, about
  1.3–1.4kg, jointed
sea salt and black pepper
4 leeks, trimmed and
  finely sliced
1 bouquet garni (bay leaf,
  few thyme and parsley
  sprigs, tied together)
1 litre chicken stock
  (see page 243)
30g butter
200g chestnut
  mushrooms, trimmed
  and roughly sliced
200g smoked back
  bacon, derinded and
  chopped
2 tbsp plain flour
150ml double cream
small handful of flat-leaf
  parsley, leaves only,
  chopped
400g good-quality
  ready-made puff pastry
1 large egg yolk, beaten
  with 1 tbsp water,
  to glaze

You can't beat a good chicken pie for that comforting, feel-good factor. Our version includes bacon, which adds a delicious smoky element to the creamy sauce.

Season the chicken pieces and place in a pan with the leeks, bouquet garni and stock; top up with water to cover if necessary. Bring to a simmer and skim, then partially cover the pan and simmer gently for 1 hour or until the chicken is tender. Lift out and leave to cool slightly. Transfer the leeks to a large bowl, using a slotted spoon. Boil the stock vigorously until reduced by half, to about 400ml. Cut the chicken into bite-sized pieces, discarding the skin and bones. Add to the leeks.

Heat a wide pan, add the butter and fry the mushrooms with a little seasoning until golden brown. Add the bacon and fry for a few more minutes until browned. Add the flour and stir over the heat for a few minutes. Pour in the reduced stock, then the cream, and simmer until reduced to a thick coating consistency. Take off the heat and mix in the chicken and leeks. Season well, stir in the parsley and let cool.

Preheat the oven to 200°C/Gas 6. Roll out the pastry on a lightly floured surface to the thickness of a £1 coin. Using a large 1.75 litre pie dish as a template, cut out a pastry lid, slightly larger all round than your dish. Cut 2cm wide strips from the trimmings. Position a pie funnel, if using, in the centre of the dish and spoon in the filling. Brush the edge of the dish with water and lay the pastry strips on the rim, joining to fit as necessary; press down lightly. Brush the pastry rim with egg glaze.

Lift the pastry lid on top of the pie and cut a small steam hole in the middle. Press the pastry edges together to seal, trim off the excess and knock up the edges. If you like, decorate the pie with pastry leaves cut from the trimmings. Brush with a little more egg glaze. Bake for 40–50 minutes until the pastry is golden brown.

Cornish pasties

Cornish pasties are sold all over the country these days, though few ready-made versions taste like the real thing. It's well worth making them yourself, as they are delicious eaten warm from the oven. Seasoning the filling liberally with pepper is essential for an authentic flavour.

Peel the potatoes, swede and onion and cut into 1cm dice. Cut the beef into similar-sized pieces and season with a generous pinch each of salt and pepper. Heat the olive oil and half the butter in a wide frying pan over a medium-high heat. When hot, sear the beef in batches for 1–2 minutes, turning to brown all over. Transfer to a plate.

Add the remaining butter to the pan and fry the diced vegetables for 5–7 minutes until they start to soften and take on a little colour. Tip any juices from the resting beef into the pan and cook until absorbed and the vegetables are tender. Add to the beef and leave to cool.

Preheat the oven to 220°C/Gas 7. Divide the pastry into four portions. Roll out each one on a lightly floured surface to a large circle, 3–4mm thick, and trim to a neat round, 25cm in diameter, using a dinner plate as a guide. Divide the filling evenly between the rounds, sprinkling each portion with a little more salt and a generous pinch of pepper.

Brush the pastry edges with a little beaten egg, then fold one half over the meat to create a semi-circle. With your fingers, pinch and turn the edges to seal each pasty and stop the filling leaking during baking.

Transfer the pasties to a large baking sheet (preferably non-stick) and brush the tops with beaten egg. Bake for 10 minutes, then lower the oven setting to 180°C/Gas 4 and cook for a further 20–25 minutes. If the pastry appears to be over-browning, cover with greaseproof paper. Allow to cool slightly. The pasties are best eaten warm, though they can also be served at room temperature.

MAKES 4 LARGE PASTIES (TO SERVE 8)

900g shortcrust pastry (see page 248, make a triple quantity)
400g waxy potatoes, such as Charlotte or Desirée
½ swede, about 400g
1 large sweet onion
400g rump or sirloin of beef
sea salt
2 tsp coarsely ground black pepper
1 tbsp olive oil
20g butter, diced
1 medium egg, lightly beaten

Steak and kidney pie

SERVES 4

800g beef chuck or
braising steak
175g veal kidney
25g plain flour
sea salt and black pepper
50g butter, diced
250g chestnut
mushrooms, quartered
2 large onions, peeled
and chopped
2 garlic cloves, peeled
and chopped
330ml bottle Guinness or
brown ale
300ml veal or beef stock
(see page 244)
2 bay leaves
few thyme sprigs, plus
extra leaves to finish
1 tbsp tomato purée
1 tbsp Worcestershire
sauce
1–2 tbsp HP brown sauce,
to taste
bunch of flat-leaf
parsley, leaves only,
chopped
500g good-quality
ready-made puff pastry
2 medium egg yolks,
beaten with 1 tbsp
water, to glaze

This is traditional British pub grub at its finest. If you're not keen on kidney, simply replace with extra steak.

Cut the beef into 2.5cm pieces. Halve the kidney and carefully remove the sinewy core, then cut into small pieces. Season the flour with salt and pepper. Toss the steak in the flour to coat, then do the same with the kidney pieces, keeping them separate.

Heat a wide, heavy-based pan, then add a few knobs of butter and fry the mushrooms with a little seasoning for 2–3 minutes until lightly browned. Add the onions and garlic and cook until the onion begins to soften. Transfer the vegetables to a bowl and set aside.

Add a few more knobs of butter to the pan and fry the kidney for 1 minute on each side, turning until evenly browned; remove and set aside. Add little more butter to the pan and brown the steak pieces in batches; they should take about 5–6 minutes to brown all over. Return all the browned steak, kidney and vegetables to the pan and pour in the Guinness. Let it simmer until reduced by one-third.

Add the stock, bay leaves, thyme, tomato purée and Worcestershire sauce. Bring to a bare simmer, partially cover and cook very gently for 1½–2 hours until the meat is tender, giving an occasional stir.

Using a slotted spoon, transfer the meat, kidney and vegetables to a large bowl. Discard the thyme and bay leaves. Boil the liquor steadily until it has reduced to a thick coating consistency. Taste and adjust the seasoning with salt, pepper and HP sauce. Pour the sauce over the meat and vegetables, stir in the chopped parsley and leave to cool.

Preheat the oven to 200°C/Gas 6. Roll out the pastry on a lightly floured surface to the thickness of a £1 coin. Cut out 4 rectangles, large enough to top individual pie dishes. Cut 1–2cm wide strips from the trimmings.

Divide the filling between four individual pie dishes and brush the rims with water. Lay the pastry strips on the rims, joining them to fit as necessary and pressing downing lightly. Brush with water. Lift the pastry lids over the pie filling and press the edges onto the rims to seal, then trim off the excess pastry. Brush with egg glaze and sprinkle with a little sea salt. If you wish, decorate with leaves cut from the pastry trimmings and sprinkle with thyme leaves. Bake for 25–30 minutes until golden brown and piping hot.

Bosworth goat's cheese tart

Bosworth is a British, unpasteurized, matured goat's cheese with an excellent flavour. This rich and indulgent tart is best served in thin slices, with a sharply dressed salad to offset the filling of creamy goat's cheese, sweet currants and red onion marmalade – as a starter or lunch.

Roll out the pastry on a lightly floured surface to a large round, the thickness of a £1 coin. Use to line a 23cm tart tin, 2–3cm deep, with removable base, leaving a little excess overhanging the rim. Leave in the fridge to rest for at least 30 minutes.

Preheat the oven to 200°C/Gas 6. Line the tart case with baking paper and dried or ceramic baking beans and bake 'blind' for 15–20 minutes until lightly golden and set around the edges. Remove the paper and beans and bake for further 5–10 minutes to cook the pastry base. While still warm, cut off the excess pastry to level with the rim of the tin. Leave to cool slightly. Turn the oven down to 180°C/Gas 4.

Spread the red onion marmalade over the base of the pastry case. Crumble the goat's cheese into a large bowl and mix in the cream and egg yolks until evenly blended; the mixture will be quite thick and stiff. Stir in the thyme leaves and currants, and season well with salt and pepper. Spoon the mixture on top of the onion marmalade layer, smoothing the surface or swirling it with the back of a fork for a rustic effect if you like.

Bake for 25–30 minutes until the filling is lightly golden and set. Cool slightly before unmoulding. Serve warm or at room temperature.

SERVES 6–8

300g shortcrust pastry (see page 248)

1 quantity red onion marmalade (see page 247)

250g Bosworth or other good-quality goat's cheese

150ml single cream

2 large egg yolks

few thyme sprigs, leaves stripped

1½ tbsp currants

sea salt and black pepper

Montgomery cheddar and potato pie

SERVES 4

500g shortcrust pastry
  (see page 248, make a
  double quantity)
few knobs of butter
2 large onions, peeled
  and chopped
few thyme sprigs, leaves
  stripped
sea salt and black pepper
800g potatoes, such as
  Desirée or Maris Piper
200g traditional mature
  cheddar, such as
  Montgomery, grated
1 large egg yolk, beaten
  with 1 tbsp water,
  to glaze

This rustic, free-form pie is ideal if you do not have a pie tin to hand. It makes a great vegetarian lunch, especially if you serve it warm from the oven, accompanied by buttery greens or a side salad.

Melt the butter in a heavy-based pan and add the onions, thyme and some seasoning. Sweat over a medium heat, stirring occasionally, for 6–8 minutes until the onions are soft.

Meanwhile, peel the potatoes and cut into 5mm thick slices. Add to a pan of boiling salted water and blanch for 3–4 minutes until they are just tender when pierced with a knife. Drain thoroughly and place in a wide bowl. Leave to cool, then mix in the onions, cheese and a generous pinch each of salt and pepper.

Preheat the oven to 200°C/Gas 6. Divide the pastry into two pieces, one slightly larger than the other. Roll out the smaller piece of pastry on a lightly floured surface to a circle, about the size of a 25cm dinner plate. Lift onto a baking sheet. Roll out the other portion of pastry to a circle, about 5cm larger in diameter than the previous one.

Roughly layer the potato and cheese filling in the middle of the pastry round on the baking sheet, leaving a 3–4cm border. Try to stack the potato slices up against each other so that the pie will have a nice shape and somewhat straight sides. Brush the border with the egg glaze. Drape the other pastry round over the top and press down the edges to seal, taking care not to leave large air pockets in the filling.

Crimp the edges, then brush the pastry with egg glaze. If you wish, sprinkle with coarse sea salt. Bake for 45–55 minutes until the pastry is golden brown. Rest for a few minutes before slicing and serving.

Tomato, goat's cheese and herb tart

Make this tart in the summer, at the height of the tomato season, when the fruit is juicy and bursting with flavour. Serve as a starter, or lunch with a leafy salad on the side.

Roll out the pastry on a lightly floured surface to a large rectangle, about 25 x 35cm. Trim the edges to neaten, then lift onto a large baking sheet. Using a sharp knife, lightly score a 1.5cm border along the edges. Brush the border with egg glaze and chill for 30 minutes.

Meanwhile, put the olive oil and herb leaves into a blender or food processor with some salt and pepper and pulse for a few seconds until the herbs are finely chopped, but still bright green. Set aside.

Preheat the oven to 200°C/Gas 6. Thinly slice the goat's cheese and tomatoes to the same, even thickness. Remove the pastry from the fridge and brush or spread most of the herb oil over the surface, within the marked border.

Arrange the goat's cheese and tomato slices alternately on top of the pastry, overlapping them in neat rows. Drizzle the remaining herb oil over the top, then sprinkle with a little more salt and pepper. Bake the tart for 35–40 minutes until the pastry is golden brown and crisp. Leave to cool slightly, for about 5 minutes, before slicing and serving.

SERVES 4–6

500g puff pastry
1 egg yolk, beaten with
  1 tbsp water, to glaze
75ml olive oil
few sprigs each of flat-
  leaf parsley, oregano
  and basil , leaves only
sea salt and black pepper
200g goat's cheese, with
  rind
4–5 plum tomatoes

COMFORT FOOD

Toad-in-the-hole

Pig's liver faggots braised in ale

Black country beef stew

Smoked ham hock with pease pudding

Rabbit hotpot with perry

Mutton with parsley and caper sauce

Sausages with mustard mash and
  sweet and sour peppers

Pork cheeks in spices and bashed neeps

Venison stew

Lancashire hotpot

Honeyed pork stew

Cider braised ham

Beef cheeks braised in stout with dumplings

Braised neck of lamb with turnips

Toad-in-the-hole

This English classic uses mostly storecupboard ingredients and is perfect for casual weeknight suppers or times when friends stop by unexpectedly – just keep some butcher's sausages to hand in the freezer. Popular with children and adults alike, toad-in-the-hole is delicious with lashings of onion gravy and some roasted vegetables on the side.

Preheat the oven to 200°C/Gas 6. Spoon the olive oil into a 1.5 litre baking dish and tilt the dish to oil the base evenly. Add the sausages and toss well to coat. Bake in the hot oven for 10 minutes.

Meanwhile, to make the batter, put the flour, salt, eggs and milk into a blender or food processor. Blend for a couple of minutes until smooth, stopping to scrape down the sides after a minute, to loosen any clumps of flour.

Take the sausages out of the oven and pour the batter all around them. Return to the oven and bake for another 30 minutes until the batter has risen dramatically and is golden brown.

Meanwhile, make the onion gravy. Melt the butter in a saucepan and add the onions with some seasoning. Sweat over a medium heat, stirring occasionally, for about 8–10 minutes until they are soft and translucent. Add the flour and stir for another couple of minutes. Gradually stir in the stock and bring to a simmer. Add the mustard, redcurrant jam and Worcestershire sauce to taste. Simmer until the gravy has thickened to a light coating consistency. Taste and adjust the seasoning with salt and pepper.

When ready, remove the toad-in-the-hole from the oven and let stand for a few minutes before serving, with the onion gravy.

SERVES 4

2 tbsp olive oil
8 good-quality thick
  pork sausages
150g plain flour
½ tsp fine sea salt
2 large eggs
150ml milk

ONION GRAVY

20g butter
2 red onions, peeled and
  finely sliced
sea salt and black pepper
1½ tbsp plain flour
300ml chicken stock
  (see page 243)
1 tsp English mustard
2 tbsp redcurrant jam,
  to taste
few dashes of
  Worcestershire sauce

Pig's liver faggots braised in ale

Faggots may not sound too appetizing, but as long as they are properly made, they are delicious and easy to prepare. If you don't own a mincer, there's no need to invest in one for this recipe – just ask your butcher to mince the pork liver and belly for you. Bear in mind that you may need to order the caul fat from him in advance. *(Recipe overleaf)*

SERVES 6

20g butter
1 medium onion, peeled
  and finely chopped
1 garlic clove, peeled and
  finely crushed
sea salt and black pepper
⅓ tsp ground mace
⅓ tsp allspice
pinch of cayenne pepper
1 tsp chopped sage
1 tsp chopped thyme
400g pork liver, trimmed
  and minced
250g minced pork belly
125g fresh white
  breadcrumbs
150g caul fat, soaked
  in water

GRAVY

15g butter
1 medium onion, peeled
  and finely chopped
1 tbsp plain flour
½ tsp tomato purée
250ml golden ale
500ml chicken stock
  (see page 243)
few dashes of
  Worcestershire sauce

To prepare the faggots, melt the butter in a small pan and add the onion, garlic and a pinch each of salt and pepper. Sweat over a medium heat, stirring occasionally, for 6–8 minutes until the onion is soft but not coloured. Tip into a large bowl and leave to cool. Add the rest of the ingredients, except the caul fat, seasoning well. Mix until well combined.

Divide the faggot mixture into 6 portions and shape each one into a neat ball. Place them on a tray, cover with cling film and chill for at least 30 minutes to allow them to firm up.

Preheat the oven to 200°C/Gas 6. Cut the caul fat into 6 large squares and wrap one around each faggot, overlapping the ends, which should stick together. Place in a lightly oiled roasting tray, spacing the faggots slightly apart. Press gently to flatten very slightly, sprinkle with a little seasoning and bake for about 30–35 minutes until nicely browned.

While the faggots are roasting, make the gravy. Melt the butter in a heavy-based saucepan and add the onion with some seasoning. Sweat over a medium heat, stirring frequently, for 5–6 minutes until starting to soften. Stir in the flour and tomato purée to make a paste. Cook, stirring, for a minute or two, then stir in the ale, keeping the mixture smooth. Boil until the liquor has reduced by two-thirds. Pour in the stock and bring back to a simmer. Simmer for 10–15 minutes until thickened slightly. Season well to taste with salt, pepper and a few dashes of Worcestershire sauce.

Take the roasting tray from the oven and pour the sauce over the faggots to coat all of them. Bake for another 10–15 minutes until the sauce is rich and thick and the faggots are nicely glazed, basting them halfway through. Serve hot, with mushy peas.

Black country beef stew

This hearty beef stew is named after its region of origin in the Midlands, which is centred around the South Staffordshire coalfield. The addition of mushrooms and black pudding slices at the end gives another dimension. Serve with cabbage and chunks of country bread.

Cut the beef into bite-sized pieces, season the flour and toss the beef in it to coat. Heat a wide, heavy-based pan and add a thin film of olive oil. Brown the beef in batches, for about 2 minutes on each side, taking care not to overcrowd the pan. Transfer to a plate; set aside.

Add a little more oil to the pan, followed by the onion, carrot and celery. Stir in the tomato purée and a little seasoning. Sauté for 5–6 minutes until the vegetables begin to soften and colour. Return the meat to the pan and add the bouquet garni. Pour in the ale and stock.

Bring to a simmer, skim, then partially cover and turn the heat right down. Cook at a bare simmer for 3–4 hours until the beef is meltingly tender. Taste and adjust the seasoning. To thicken the stew slightly if necessary, add the arrowroot mixture and simmer for a few minutes.

Heat a wide frying pan with a thin layer of olive oil. Fry the black pudding and mushrooms separately, each with a little seasoning, until evenly browned. Add to the stew and serve with a sprinkling of chives.

SERVES 4

800g braising beef or
  beef skirt
2 tbsp plain flour
sea salt and black pepper
3–4 tbsp olive oil
1 large onion, peeled and
  chopped
1 carrot, peeled and
  chopped
1 celery stick, trimmed
  and chopped
1 tbsp tomato purée
1 bouquet garni (bay leaf,
  few parsley, sage and
  thyme sprigs, tied
  together)
500ml pale ale
300ml beef stock
  (see page 244)
1½ tsp arrowroot mixed
  with 1 tbsp water
  (optional)
225g black pudding, cut
  into bite-sized pieces
125g chestnut
  mushrooms, trimmed
  and sliced
handful of chives,
  chopped

Smoked ham hock with pease pudding

SERVES 4

1 large smoked ham hock
  with bone, about 1.2kg,
  soaked overnight in
  plenty of cold water
2 leeks, trimmed
2 celery sticks, trimmed
1 large carrot, peeled
1 large onion, peeled and
  halved
1 head of garlic, halved
  horizontally
2 bay leaves
few thyme sprigs
few rosemary sprigs
1 tsp black peppercorns

PEASE PUDDING

300g split green peas,
  soaked overnight in
  cold water
1 small onion, peeled and
  finely chopped
1 tbsp butter
few dashes of
  Worcestershire sauce
black pepper
small bunch of flat-leaf
  parsley, leaves chopped

This is a fantastic recipe for a crowd – simply poach another ham hock in the stock, using the same amount of flavouring vegetables, and double the pease pudding. The whole dish can be cooked in advance but you'll need to plan ahead as both the ham hock and split peas require overnight soaking.

Rinse and drain the ham hock, then put it into a large pan. Cut the leeks, celery and carrot into 5cm lengths and add to the pan with the onion, garlic, herbs and peppercorns. Pour in enough cold water to cover. Bring to the boil, then skim off any scum from the surface. Cover with a lid and gently simmer for 2–3 hours, until the meat is tender and comes away from the bone easily.

Remove the ham hock from the poaching liquor and set aside to cool slightly. When cool enough to handle, flake the meat into large pieces, discarding the skin and bones. Measure out 600ml of the stock for the peas (save the rest – you can use it to make London particular, see page 69).

For the pease pudding, drain the split peas and put them into a saucepan with the chopped onion. Pour in the poaching stock and bring to a simmer, then cover and cook for about 2½–3 hours until the peas are soft and the liquid has mostly been absorbed. Add the butter and Worcestershire sauce and season well with black pepper. For a smoother result, use a hand-held stick blender to work the peas to a coarse-textured purée.

When ready to serve, warm the ham pieces gently if necessary in a little of the reserved stock. Serve the pease pudding piping hot in warm bowls with the flaked ham hock pieces on top. Add a sprinkling of chopped parsley to finish.

Rabbit hotpot with perry

SERVES 4–6

1 rabbit, about 1.2kg,
  jointed
2 tbsp plain flour
sea salt and black pepper
2 tbsp olive oil
20g butter
2 onions, peeled and
  chopped
2 bay leaves
few thyme sprigs
500g parsnips, peeled
  and cut into chunks
500ml perry (pear cider),
  or apple cider
about 500ml water
60g pitted prunes,
  chopped
400g tin butter or
  haricot beans, drained
2 tbsp wholegrain
  mustard
small handful of flat-leaf
  parsley, chopped

This is a particularly good dish for anyone who has never tried rabbit before. With this in mind, we've used farmed rabbit for a milder flavour, but of course you may prefer the richer, gamier taste of wild rabbit. The latter will take longer to cook, as the animals get more exercise and their meat is slower to tenderize. Get your butcher to prepare and joint the rabbit for you. Grainy mustard mash (see page 156) is the ideal accompaniment for this dish.

Preheat the oven to 180°C/Gas 4. Heat a large flameproof casserole until hot. Meanwhile, coat the rabbit pieces in the flour seasoned with salt and pepper, saving any excess. Add the olive oil to the casserole and fry the rabbit pieces, in batches if necessary, for 2 minutes on each side until golden brown all over. Remove the browned pieces to a plate and set aside.

Add the butter to the casserole. When melted, add the onions with some seasoning and sauté over a high heat for 5–6 minutes until they start to colour. Tip in any remaining seasoned flour and cook, stirring, for another couple of minutes. Add the bay leaves, thyme, parsnips and a little more seasoning. Return the rabbit to the casserole and pour in the perry and enough water to cover. Bring to a simmer, put the lid on and then carefully transfer to the oven.

Cook for 40 minutes, then take out the casserole and stir in the prunes, butter beans and mustard. Return to the oven for another 25–30 minutes until the rabbit is tender. If the sauce seems too thin, lift out the rabbit pieces and boil the sauce vigorously until reduced and thickened to a light coating consistency. Taste and adjust the seasoning. Sprinkle with chopped parsley to serve.

Mutton with parsley and caper sauce

Boiled leg of lamb is a classic dish, but we prefer to use mutton as it has a deeper flavour that is well retained during long, slow cooking. Boiling, of course, is something of a misnomer, as the cooking liquor should barely simmer, to ensure that the meat is meltingly tender. You may have to order the mutton in advance from your butcher. Failing that, you could use a boned and rolled leg of lamb.

Put the mutton into a large cooking pot and add enough cold water to cover. Bring to the boil, then turn the heat down to a simmer. Skim off the froth and scum from the surface of the liquid. Add the herbs, peppercorns and a generous pinch of salt, then simmer for 2½–3 hours until the meat is just tender.

In the meantime, cut the vegetables into small chunks. Add them to the cooking pot and return to a simmer. Cook gently for a further 40–50 minutes until the vegetables are just tender.

To make the sauce, melt the butter in a heavy-based saucepan and stir in the flour. Cook, stirring, over a medium heat for a couple of minutes. Take the pan off the heat and slowly stir in the milk, keeping the sauce smooth. Add a few ladlefuls of stock from the mutton, about 300ml, stirring well. Simmer gently for about 15 minutes, stirring frequently, until the sauce has thickened to a light coating consistency. Add the capers and parsley and season well to taste.

When ready, lift the mutton out of the stock onto a warm platter. Cover loosely with foil and leave to rest in a warm place for about 15 minutes. Carve into thin slices and serve with the vegetables and caper sauce. The mutton stock and any leftover meat and vegetables can be used to make a lovely soup.

SERVES 6

1.2kg boned and rolled
  leg of mutton
2 bay leaves
few thyme sprigs
1 tsp black peppercorns
sea salt
2 large leeks, trimmed
2–3 large carrots, peeled
1 large swede, about
  400–450g, peeled
2 medium turnips, about
  400–450g, peeled

PARSLEY AND CAPER SAUCE

45g butter
3 tbsp plain flour
300ml warm milk
5–6 tbsp capers, rinsed
small bunch of flat-leaf
  parsley, leaves chopped
sea salt and black pepper

Sausages with mustard mash and sweet and sour peppers

SERVES 4
8 good-quality pork
  sausages, such as
  Gloucester Old Spot
1½ tbsp olive oil

MUSTARD MASH
1kg floury potatoes, such
  as Maris Piper or King
  Edward, peeled
150ml double cream
75ml milk
75g butter, diced
2½ tbsp wholegrain
  mustard
sea salt and black pepper

SWEET AND SOUR
PEPPERS
2 large red peppers,
  trimmed, deseeded and
  finely sliced
1½ tbsp olive oil
few thyme sprigs
little splash of red wine
  vinegar, such as
  Cabernet Sauvignon
pinch of caster sugar
  (optional)

Most of the sausages we serve in the pubs are made from free-range Old Spot pork. One of the oldest pedigree pig breeds, Old Spot has a superlative flavour, often attributed to diet. The pigs graze greedily on fallen apples around the orchards in Gloucestershire, earning them the moniker, 'pigs with inbuilt apple sauce'.

For the mash, cut the potatoes into even chunks. Add to a pan of salted water, bring to the boil and cook for 15–20 minutes until tender.

Meanwhile, cook the sausages. Heat the olive oil in a wide, non-stick frying pan over a medium-low heat, then fry the sausages gently for 15–20 minutes until cooked, turning frequently to ensure that they brown evenly. (Don't pierce the skins or you'll lose some of the juices.)

While the sausages are cooking, sauté the peppers. Heat another frying pan until hot, then add the olive oil, thyme, red peppers and some seasoning. Toss the peppers frequently for 4–5 minutes until starting to soften. Add the wine vinegar, toss well and cook until the pan is quite dry. Taste and adjust the seasoning, adding a pinch of sugar, if necessary, though the peppers should be sweet enough.

When the potatoes are cooked, drain them well and return to the pan to dry out for a minute or two. Pass through a potato ricer back into the pan or mash well. Warm the cream, milk and butter in a pan over a low heat until the butter has melted, then take off the heat and slowly stir into the mashed potato. Stir in the mustard and season with salt and pepper to taste.

Serve two sausages per person on a pile of grainy mash with the sweet and sour peppers on the side.

Pork cheeks in spices and bashed neeps

This lovely dish of meltingly tender pork cheeks coated in a rich, sweet gravy is inexpensive, yet smart enough for a dinner party. It is delicious with buttery swede, or 'bashed neeps', and creamy mash. You may need to order the pork from your butcher in advance.

Preheat the oven to 150°C/Gas 2. Trim away any large pieces of fat from the pork cheeks and cut each cheek into two or three smaller pieces. Heat the olive oil in a large frying pan until hot. Season the pork cheeks all over with salt and pepper and fry for about 2 minutes on each side. Add a knob of butter to finish off the browning. Transfer to a plate.

Add the onion, carrot and celery to the frying pan and fry for 6–8 minutes until softened and caramelized to a rich golden brown colour. Stir in the tomato purée and fry for a further minute. Add the honey, cloves and star anise and increase the heat slightly. When bubbling, remove from the heat and tip the contents into a casserole dish.

Add the browned pork cheeks with any juices, the herbs, and the hot stock to cover. Cover the casserole and place in the oven. Braise for 2–2½ hours until the meat is very tender and starting to fall apart.

Half an hour before the pork will be ready, prepare the bashed neeps. Add the swede to a pan of salted water, bring to the boil and cook for 25–30 minutes until tender. Drain well, then mash and beat in the butter. Season well with salt, pepper and nutmeg to taste. Keep warm.

When ready, remove the pork cheeks from the casserole with a slotted spoon to a bowl. Strain the sauce through a sieve into a pan, pushing down on the vegetables to extract all the juices. Boil vigorously until reduced by about two-thirds and thickened to a syrupy consistency. Check the seasoning. Return the pork cheeks to the sauce to reheat. Serve on warm plates, with the bashed neeps.

SERVES 4–6

1.4kg pork cheeks, skin removed
2 tbsp olive oil
sea salt and black pepper
2–3 knobs of butter
1 onion, peeled and chopped
1 large carrot, peeled and chopped
2 celery sticks, trimmed and chopped
1 tbsp tomato purée
175ml clear honey
1 tsp cloves
1 star anise
few thyme sprigs
2 bay leaves
750ml boiling chicken stock (see page 243)

BASHED NEEPS

650g swede, peeled and chopped
40g butter
freshly grated nutmeg

Venison stew

SERVES 4

1kg venison shoulder

½ tsp juniper berries,
  lightly crushed

1 tsp black peppercorns

few thyme sprigs

few rosemary sprigs

1 bay leaf

300ml red wine

300ml port

2 tbsp plain flour

sea salt and black pepper

2–3 tbsp olive oil

200g piece of smoked
  streaky bacon, derinded

2 onions, peeled and
  finely chopped

600ml beef or veal stock
  (see page 244)

250g small chestnut or
  button mushrooms,
  halved

flat-leaf parsley leaves,
  roughly torn, to finish

Venison is a fantastic lean meat that can easily dry out during cooking. Although it is not absolutely essential, marinating the venison in port, wine and spices certainly helps to keep it moist, while imparting a dark, rich colour and extra flavour to the meat.

Cut the venison into bite-sized pieces and place in a large bowl with the juniper berries, peppercorns and herbs. Pour over the red wine and port, then cover the bowl with cling film and leave to marinate in the fridge overnight.

The next day, lift the venison out of the marinade and pat dry with kitchen paper; reserve the marinade. Season the flour with salt and pepper, then use to coat the venison pieces. Heat a large flameproof casserole and add a thin layer of olive oil. When hot, fry the venison in several batches, for 2 minutes on each side until browned all over. Remove to a plate with a slotted spoon.

Cut the bacon into chunks. Add a little more oil to the casserole and fry the bacon for 3–4 minutes until golden brown. Add the onions with some seasoning and stir well. Fry for another 4–6 minutes until the onions are lightly golden and beginning to soften. Pour in the marinade, including the herbs, peppercorns and juniper berries, and bring to the boil. Boil until the liquid has reduced by two-thirds.

Return the venison to the casserole and pour in the stock to cover. Turn the heat down to the lowest setting. Partially cover with the lid and cook the stew gently at a bare simmer for 1½–2 hours until the venison is just tender.

Add the mushrooms to the stew. Season well and simmer for a further 30 minutes or until the mushrooms are cooked and the sauce has thickened. Spoon into warm bowls, scatter over the parsley and serve.

Lancashire hotpot

During the industrial times, long working days for men and women left little time to devote to cooking. Meat, vegetables and potatoes were often piled into pots and left to cook all day in a low oven. A welcome return after a hard day's work, this hotpot soon became a staple in Lancashire.

Preheat the oven to 170°C/Gas 3. Cut the lamb into chops, about 2cm thick, trimming off any fat. Season the flour with salt and pepper and use to dust the chops lightly. If using kidneys, halve them and snip out the core with a pair of kitchen scissors, then cut each half in two.

Heat half the olive oil in a wide frying pan and fry the lamb in batches, for 2 minutes on each side or until evenly browned all over. Remove with a slotted spoon to a plate. Dust the kidneys in seasoned flour and fry for 1½ minutes on each side until browned; transfer to the plate.

Add a little more oil to the pan and fry the onion, carrots and garlic with a little seasoning for about 4–5 minutes until lightly browned. Tip in any remaining seasoned flour and fry for another minute or so. Pour the stock into the pan, stirring, and add the thyme and rosemary. Simmer for 5–10 minutes, then take the pan off the heat.

Assemble the hotpot in a buttered, deep casserole dish. Layer the meat, browned vegetables and sauce in the dish, seasoning well between each layer. Top with two or three layers of neatly overlapping potato slices, brushing each layer with butter and seasoning well.

Cook in the oven for about 1½–2 hours until the meat is tender and the potatoes are golden brown and crisp around the edges. To check, insert a thin skewer through the potatoes and meat; it should meet with little resistance. If the potatoes appear to be browning too quickly in the oven, cover loosely with a piece of foil. Leave the hotpot to stand for 10–15 minutes before serving.

SERVES 4–6

1kg best end of lamb
3 tbsp plain flour
sea salt and black pepper
3 lamb's kidneys (optional)
3 tbsp olive oil
1 large onion, peeled and thinly sliced
2 large carrots, peeled and thinly sliced
1 garlic clove, peeled and chopped
700ml lamb stock (see page 245)
few thyme sprigs, leaves stripped
1 or 2 rosemary sprigs, leaves only, finely chopped
700g floury potatoes, such as Maris Piper or King Edward, peeled and thinly sliced
30g butter, melted

Honeyed pork stew

SERVES 4–6

1–1.2kg boneless pork belly (ideally a leaner piece)

sea salt and black pepper

1–1½ tbsp olive oil

200g dried haricot beans, soaked overnight in cold water

500ml medium cider

600ml chicken stock (see page 243)

1 small onion, peeled

8 cloves

1 tbsp tomato purée

4–5 tbsp honey

2 tbsp Worcestershire sauce

1 bouquet garni (bay leaf, few thyme and parsley sprigs, tied together)

2 leeks, trimmed

1 celery stick, trimmed

3 medium carrots, peeled

This wonderful one-pot stew is the perfect winter warmer. Pork belly lends itself to a sweet and slightly tart sauce, which helps to counteract the richness of the meat. Serve with warm bread to soak up the tasty sauce.

Remove and discard the rind from the pork belly. Cut the meat into bite-sized cubes and season with salt and pepper. Heat the olive oil in a flameproof casserole and brown the pork in several batches, allowing about 1½–2 minutes on each side.

Drain the haricot beans and place in the casserole. Return all the browned meat, then pour in the cider and stock. Bring to a simmer and skim off the scum that rises to the surface. Add the onion studded with the cloves, the tomato purée, honey, Worcestershire sauce and bouquet garni.

Partially cover the pan with a lid and simmer slowly for 2–2½ hours until the beans and pork are just tender, giving the mixture an occasional stir.

Thinly slice the leeks and celery, and slice the carrots into rounds. Skim off the fat from the surface of the stew, then add the vegetables with some seasoning. Give the mixture a stir. Simmer for another 20–30 minutes until the vegetables are just tender. Check the seasoning before serving.

Cider braised ham

SERVES 8
2kg unsmoked boneless
  gammon, soaked
  overnight
1 onion, peeled and
  roughly chopped
1 carrot, peeled and
  roughly chopped
1 leek, trimmed and
  roughly chopped
2 bay leaves
1 tsp black peppercorns
1 litre medium cider
small handful of cloves

GLAZE
60ml honey
2 tbsp Dijon mustard
1 tbsp Worcestershire
  sauce
60g dark muscovado
  sugar

Don't just think of baked whole gammon as a dish for the festive season. Our easy cider braised ham can be enjoyed at any time of the year and it makes a lovely main course for Sunday lunch. Suitable accompaniments include glazed carrots and parsnips, and roasted or mashed sweet potatoes. Any leftover ham will be delicious served cold with salad and pickles.

Drain the gammon and put into a large cooking pot. Add enough cold water to cover and slowly bring to the boil. Simmer for a few minutes, then carefully pour off the water along with the froth from the surface.

Add the vegetables, bay leaves and peppercorns to the ham in the pot. Pour in the cider and top up with cold water to cover. Bring to a simmer, partially cover and cook gently, for 2½–3 hours, skimming frequently and topping up with boiling water as necessary.

Take the ham out of the pan and rest on a board until cool enough to handle. (If the cooking liquor is not too salty, save it and use to make London particular, see page 69). Preheat the oven to 190°C/Gas 5.

Peel off the skin from the ham and cut away some of the fat, if necessary, to leave a thin even layer. Using a sharp knife, score the fat in a criss-cross pattern, at about 1.5cm intervals. Stud each diamond with a clove. Place the ham in a large roasting pan. Mix together the ingredients for the glaze and brush over the ham. Roast for 20–25 minutes until nicely browned, basting halfway through.

As you take the ham from the oven, brush with a little more glaze, cover with foil and leave to rest for 30 minutes (in a warm place if serving the ham hot). Carve into thin slices and serve with vegetables of your choice.

Beef cheeks braised in stout with dumplings

Stout gives this rich, dark stew a lovely deep colour and flavour, and the herby horseradish dumplings go perfectly.

Trim off any excess fat from the cheeks and cut into bite-sized pieces. Mix the flour with a little salt and pepper and use to lightly coat the beef pieces. Heat a thin layer of olive oil in a heavy-based flameproof casserole. Brown the beef in batches for 4–6 minutes, turning to colour evenly, then remove to a plate.

Drizzle a little more oil into the pan and add the vegetables, along with the bay leaves and thyme. Stir in the tomato purée and sugar. Cook, stirring frequently, over a high heat for 6–8 minutes until the vegetables begin to soften and colour.

Pour in the stout and let bubble for 5–10 minutes until reduced by about half. Return the meat to the pan. Add the stock to cover the meat and vegetables. Season well, bring to the boil and put the lid on. Simmer gently for 3–3½ hours until the beef is just tender, stirring every once in a while. Taste and adjust the seasoning.

Meanwhile, to make the dumplings, put the flour, suet, salt and a good pinch of pepper into a large bowl. Mix well, then stir in the chopped herbs. Make a well in the centre and add the creamed horseradish and 4 tbsp water. Mix to a firm dough that comes away from the sides of the bowl cleanly. If it is a bit dry, add a little more water. Turn the dough out onto a clean board and sprinkle over some flour. Roll the dough out into a sausage shape, then divide into 8 balls.

Carefully drop the dumplings into the stew, spacing them apart to allow for them to double in size during cooking. Replace the lid and cook for a further 20–30 minutes until the dumplings have puffed up and are light and fluffy. Serve with seasonal vegetables.

SERVES 4

2 beef cheeks, about 500g each
2 tbsp plain flour
sea salt and black pepper
2–3 tbsp olive oil
1 large carrot, peeled and chopped
1 celery stick, trimmed and chopped
1 leek, trimmed and chopped
2 bay leaves
few thyme sprigs
1 tbsp tomato purée
1 tbsp brown sugar
300ml Guinness or other stout
400ml beef or veal stock (see page 244)

DUMPLINGS

125g self-raising flour
125g suet
½ tsp salt
small handful of mixed herbs, such as parsley, chives and chervil, chopped
1 heaped tsp creamed horseradish
4–5 tbsp water

Braised neck of lamb
with turnips

SERVES 4

1kg neck of lamb fillet

3 tbsp plain flour

sea salt and black pepper

2–3 tbsp olive oil

1 large onion, peeled and
  chopped

600g turnips, peeled and
  cut into small chunks

splash of sherry

few thyme sprigs

1 bay leaf

1 litre lamb stock
  (see page 245)

small handful of flat-leaf
  parsley, leaves only,
  chopped

Featuring neck of lamb, an economical cut well suited to slow braising, this is a wonderfully comforting stew for wintry days. We also like to serve it in the spring when we add a selection of spring vegetables, such as baby turnips, young carrots, fresh peas and broad beans – towards the end of cooking to retain their vibrant colours and flavours.

Cut the lamb into bite-sized pieces, then lightly coat them in the flour seasoned with a little salt and pepper. Heat a wide frying pan and add a thin layer of olive oil. Fry the lamb pieces in several batches until evenly browned all over. Remove to a plate, using a slotted spoon.

Add a little more oil to the pan as necessary and tip in the onion and turnips. Add a pinch of seasoning and fry over a high heat for 4–6 minutes until the vegetables take on a little colour. Pour in a splash of sherry and let it bubble down to a glaze.

Return the lamb to the pan and add the thyme sprigs, bay leaf, and the stock to cover. Bring to a simmer and skim off the froth and scum from the surface. Partially cover the pan with a lid and simmer for 2–3 hours until the lamb is tender.

If the sauce is too thin, strain the liquid into a wide saucepan and boil until reduced and thickened to a light coating consistency. Season well to taste. Add the lamb and vegetables to the sauce to reheat for a couple of minutes. Sprinkle with the chopped parsley and serve.

GRILLS AND SAUTES

Gammon steak with pineapple and fried duck egg

Marinated chicken with minted broad beans and peas

Barnsley chop with kidneys

Lamb steak with redcurrant sauce

Citrus spatchcocked quail with sautéed potatoes

Veal escalope with asparagus and mushrooms

Rib-eye steak with chips and sauce choron

Sirloin steak with green peppercorn sauce

Liver, bacon and caramelized onions

Pork chop with champ

Gammon steak with
pineapple and fried duck egg

SERVES 4

1 medium pineapple

4 thin gammon steaks, about 150–200g each

few knobs of butter, plus extra melted for brushing

a little caster sugar, to sprinkle

2 tbsp olive oil or duck fat

4 duck eggs

black pepper

Grilled gammon steak and pineapple is a classic pairing, but our version of this dish includes a duck egg with its deliciously rich, creamy yolk. Eaten together, it's our idea of heaven on a fork.

To prepare the pineapple, slice off the top and the bottom and then stand it upright on a board. Cut away the skin, following the curve of the fruit, and remove any remaining 'black eyes' with the tip of your knife. Turn the pineapple on its side and cut into 1cm thick slices. Remove the core, using an apple corer or a small pastry cutter. You need 4 neat slices. (Save the rest for a fruit salad or eat as a snack.)

Preheat the grill to its highest setting. If you wish, remove the rind from the gammon, leaving a layer of fat surrounding each steak. Snip the fat with kitchen scissors at 2cm intervals all around, to prevent the steaks from curling up as they cook. Brush the steaks on both sides with melted butter and lay them on the grill pan rack. Grill for 3–4 minutes on each side, or until the gammon is cooked through and the fat is golden brown and crisp. Keep warm.

Meanwhile, set two wide frying pans over a medium heat. Melt a few knobs of butter in one frying pan. Sprinkle the pineapple rings with caster sugar and fry for 3–4 minutes on each side until golden brown and caramelized. At the same time, heat the olive oil or duck fat in the other pan, carefully crack in the duck eggs and fry until the whites are set but the yolks are still runny in the middle. (You may need to cook them in two batches if your pan is not large enough.)

Put a gammon steak on each warm plate and top with a pineapple ring and a fried duck egg. Grind some black pepper over the eggs and serve immediately.

Marinated chicken with
minted broad beans and peas

This is a fantastic, colourful dish for spring, when fresh peas and broad beans are abundant, sweet and tender.

Put the chicken into a bowl with the lemon zest, crushed seeds and pepper, herbs, olive oil and a good pinch of salt. Toss to coat, then cover and leave to marinate in the fridge for a few hours, or overnight.

For the herb butter, in a bowl, beat the butter with the chopped herbs and some seasoning until well blended. Shape into a log on a piece of cling film and wrap in the film. Chill in the fridge until firm.

Blanch the broad beans in a pan of boiling salted water for 3–4 minutes until tender. With a slotted spoon, transfer to a bowl of iced water to refresh, then drain. Add the peas to the pan and blanch for 3 minutes, then refresh in iced water and drain. Slip the broad beans out of their skins. Place them in a bowl with the peas and set aside.

When ready to cook, preheat the oven to 180°C/Gas 4. Place a wide ovenproof frying pan over a medium-high heat. Lift the chicken out of the marinade into the hot pan and fry, skin side down, for 2–3 minutes until golden brown and crisp. Add the thyme and rosemary sprigs to the pan. Turn the chicken breasts over and fry the underside for 2–3 minutes until golden brown. Flip the chicken breasts again and place the pan in the oven for 10–12 minutes or until the chicken is just cooked through; it should feel just firm when lightly pressed. Leave to rest in a warm place while you reheat the peas and broad beans.

Melt the butter in a pan and throw in the peas, broad beans and mint. Add a splash of hot water and simmer for a minute or so until hot. Season to taste and divide among warm plates. Lay a chicken supreme on each plate and garnish with the thyme and rosemary. Top each chicken portion with a thick slice of herb butter and serve at once.

SERVES 4

4 chicken supremes
  (breast with skin and
  wing tip attached),
  about 200–225g each
finely pared zest of
  2 lemons
1 tsp coriander seeds,
  lightly crushed
1 tsp black peppercorns,
  lightly crushed
few rosemary sprigs
few thyme sprigs
100ml olive oil
sea salt and black pepper

HERB BUTTER

50g butter, softened
½ tsp chopped tarragon
½ tsp chopped chervil or
  flat-leaf parsley

BROAD BEANS AND PEAS

200g podded fresh or
  frozen broad beans,
  thawed if frozen
150g podded fresh or
  frozen peas, thawed if
  frozen
few knobs of butter
few mint sprigs, leaves
  only, chopped

Barnsley chop
with kidneys

SERVES 4

4 Barnsley chops, about
  300–350g each
4 lamb's kidneys
3 tbsp olive oil
sea salt and black pepper
small bunch of
  watercress, to garnish

If you're not familiar with them, Barnsley chops are cut across the saddle of lamb, to give two joined pieces of loin separated by a bone in the middle. Buy good-quality chops, ideally from rare-breed lamb, and you'll appreciate the full flavour of prime meat cooked on the bone. And, of course, make sure the kidneys are very fresh. Braised red cabbage (see page 199) and chips are perfect accompaniments.

Trim off the excess fat around the chops, leaving an even layer surrounding them, and set aside. Halve the lamb's kidneys and snip out the white cores with a pair of kitchen scissors.

Heat half the olive oil in a large frying pan (or use two smaller frying pans simultaneously). Season the chops with salt and pepper and fry over a medium-high heat for 2½–3 minutes on each side, spooning the pan juices over them as they cook. If the band of fat around each chop is not sufficiently crisp, hold the chops upright with tongs to fry the fat until golden brown and crisp. The chops are ready when the meat feels slightly springy if lightly pressed. Transfer to a warm plate and leave to rest in a warm place while you cook the kidneys.

Season the kidneys with salt and pepper. Heat the remaining oil in the frying pan you cooked the chops in. Add the kidneys and fry for about 1 minute on each side, basting them with the pan juices as they cook. The kidneys are ready when nicely browned on the outside, but still pink and succulent within. Transfer them to a plate lined with kitchen paper to soak up the excess oil.

Serve immediately, placing a Barnsley chop and two kidney halves on each warm plate. Spoon over the pan juices and garnish with a handful of watercress.

Lamb steak with redcurrant sauce

This is an excellent, quick and easy way to cook lamb leg or shoulder steaks. We've used redcurrant jelly to add a little sweetness to the sauce, but you can also throw in a handful of fresh redcurrants to add a tart element: cook the redcurrants until they burst and add a little more redcurrant jelly, balancing the sweet, sour and savoury flavours; sieve the sauce before serving.

First, make the sauce. Melt the butter in a saucepan and sauté the shallot with a pinch of salt and pepper for 5–6 minutes until soft but not coloured. Add the rosemary and pour in the red wine. Let bubble until the wine has reduced by half, then pour in the stock. Return to the boil and cook until reduced again by half. Stir in the redcurrant jelly and Worcestershire sauce and adjust the seasoning to taste.

When ready to cook, season the lamb steaks on both sides with salt and pepper. Heat the olive oil in a wide frying pan, add the rosemary sprig and swirl the oil around the pan to infuse. When it is hot, add the lamb steaks and fry for 1½–2 minutes on each side until browned on the outside but still pink in the middle. They should feel slightly springy when pressed. Transfer to a warm plate and leave to rest for 3–5 minutes.

Leaving the frying pan on the heat, pour in the redcurrant sauce, scraping up any sediment from the base of the pan with a wooden spatula. Pour in any juices from the resting steaks and swirl the pan to incorporate them. Take off the heat and check the seasoning.

Place a lamb steak on each warm plate and spoon over the redcurrant sauce. Delicious with sautéed potatoes flavoured with rosemary and buttered green beans on the side.

SERVES 4
4 lamb steaks, about
 175–200g each
sea salt and black pepper
2 tbsp olive oil
1 rosemary sprig

REDCURRANT SAUCE
20g butter
1 shallot, peeled and
 finely sliced
1 rosemary sprig, leaves
 stripped and chopped
250ml red wine
250ml lamb stock (see
 page 245) or chicken
 stock (see page 243)
1 tbsp redcurrant jelly
1 tbsp Worcestershire
 sauce

Citrus spatchcocked quail with sautéed potatoes

SERVES 4

8 oven-ready quails
2–3 tbsp olive oil
finely grated zest of
  1 orange
sea salt and black pepper

CITRUS DRESSING

1 large orange
1 yellow grapefruit
1 pink grapefruit
3–4 tbsp olive oil
pinch of caster sugar

SAUTÉED POTATOES

600g waxy potatoes,
  such as baby Charlotte
1–2 tbsp olive oil
few knobs of butter
few flat-leaf parsley
  sprigs, leaves finely
  chopped

Tender quails take little time to cook, especially if they've been spatchcocked. It is easy enough to do this yourself, but getting your butcher to do it for you will save time.

To spatchcock each quail, cut along both sides of the backbone with poultry shears to remove it. Open out the bird, skin side up, on a board and press down firmly with the palm of your hand to flatten. Thread two long skewers crosswise through the quail, piercing through the legs and breasts; this helps to keep it flat. Mix the olive oil with the orange zest and some seasoning and brush over the spatchcocked quails. Put them on a tray, cover and chill until ready to cook.

For the dressing, prepare all the fruit: cut off the top and bottom and slice off the skin and pith, following the curve. Hold over a sieve set on a bowl and cut along the membranes to release the segments. Remove any pips and cut the segments into smaller pieces. Mix the collected juice with the olive oil, a pinch of sugar and seasoning to taste.

About 15 minutes before serving, heat the oven to low. Peel the potatoes and slice thinly. Heat the olive oil and butter in a large frying pan until it begins to foam. Season the potato slices and fry, in batches if necessary, for about 2 minutes on each side until golden brown and tender. Remove to a plate and keep warm in the oven.

Wipe out the pan with kitchen paper and return to the heat. Cook the quails in batches: fry them skin side down first for about 3 minutes until golden brown and the skin is crisp. Turn and cook on the other side for 2–3 minutes. Keep warm in the oven while you cook the rest.

Put two quails on each warm plate, removing the skewers. Pile the sautéed potatoes alongside and sprinkle with chopped parsley. Spoon the citrus segments and a little dressing around the quails and serve.

Veal escalope
with asparagus and mushrooms

This incredibly tasty yet simple dish is smart enough for a dinner party. Unlike the continental white veal, British rosé veal comes from dairy cattle that are humanely reared in the UK. The pale pink meat is tender, delicately flavoured and absolutely delicious pan-fried.

Pat the veal escalopes dry with kitchen paper and set aside. Bring a pot of salted water to the boil. Peel the lower part of the asparagus stalks, then add to the boiling salted water and blanch for 2–3 minutes until just tender. Lift the spears out with a pair of tongs and plunge them into a bowl of iced water to stop the cooking process. Drain again and set aside.

Heat 1 tbsp olive oil in a wide pan until hot. Add the mushrooms, thyme leaves and a good pinch each of salt and pepper. Add a few knobs of butter to the pan and fry the mushrooms for 2–3 minutes until golden brown and any moisture released has been cooked off. Add the cream and stir well to mix. Cook for a few seconds, then turn off the heat and keep warm.

Season the veal escalopes with salt and pepper. Heat a wide frying pan until very hot and add the remaining olive oil. In two batches, sear the veal over a high heat for about 30 seconds on each side until golden brown and slightly springy when gently pressed. Transfer to a warm plate and keep warm while you fry the rest of the veal.

Reheat the asparagus in simmering water for a minute, then drain. Place a veal escalope on each warm plate and arrange the asparagus alongside. Spoon over the creamed mushrooms and serve.

SERVES 4

4 thin British rosé veal escalopes, about 150–170g each

500g asparagus, trimmed

2 tbsp olive oil

500g mixed mushrooms, such as chestnut, St. George's and ceps, sliced

1 thyme sprig, leaves stripped

sea salt and black pepper

few knobs of butter

2–3 tbsp double cream

Rib-eye steak

with chips and sauce choron

SERVES 4
4 boneless rib-eye steaks,
  about 200–225g each
sea salt and black pepper
1½ tbsp olive oil
knob of butter

CHIPS
1kg floury potatoes,
  such as Maris Piper or
  King Edward
groundnut or vegetable
  oil, for deep-frying

SAUCE CHORON
100ml lemon and
  tarragon hollandaise
  (see page 246)
knob of butter
1 shallot, peeled and
  finely chopped
1 garlic clove, peeled and
  finely chopped
1 large plum tomato,
  skinned, deseeded and
  diced

This is one of our most popular items on the pub menus. A rib-eye steak has a beautiful marbling of creamy fat, mostly centred on the middle (or the 'eye') of the rib steak, which melts, bastes and flavours the meat as it cooks.

First, prepare the chips. Peel the potatoes and cut into 1–1.5cm wedges. Add to a pan of cold salted water, bring to the boil, then immediately take the pan off the heat. Leave the potatoes in the cooking water for 3–4 minutes, then drain well in a colander and leave to dry out.

Heat the oil for deep-frying in a deep-fryer or other suitable pan to 120°C. Put the potatoes into a chip basket and immerse in the hot oil. Deep-fry for 5–7 minutes until they are cooked through and lightly golden on the outside. Drain on a tray lined with kitchen paper.

For the sauce, have the hollandaise ready. Melt the butter in a small pan and gently sweat the shallot and garlic with some seasoning for 5–6 minutes until soft but not coloured. Add the tomato and cook for 30 seconds. Transfer to a bowl and stir in the hollandaise. Keep warm by standing the bowl in a pan of hot water; stir occasionally.

Reheat the oil to 190°C and fry the chips for a second time, for 3–5 minutes until golden brown and crisp. Drain on kitchen paper and sprinkle with salt. Keep crisp in a low oven while you cook the steaks.

Heat a wide frying pan until very hot. Season the steaks well with salt and pepper. Add a swirl of oil to the pan and fry the steaks for 1½–2½ minutes on each side, depending on thickness, until the outside is nicely browned but the meat is still medium rare. They should feel slightly springy when pressed. (For medium steaks, cook for a minute longer.) Transfer to warm plates and rest for a couple of minutes, before serving, with the chips and sauce choron on the side.

Sirloin steak with green peppercorn sauce

This succulent steak comes with a double dose of peppers, in the form of cracked black peppercorns on the meat and mild green peppercorns in the sauce. Serve with potatoes, cooked any way you like, and a leafy green salad tossed in a mustardy dressing.

To prepare the steaks, lightly crush the black peppercorns with a pestle and mortar, then sift out the fine dust. Tip the crushed peppercorns onto a plate. Season both sides of the steaks with salt, then coat with the crushed peppercorns.

Heat a wide frying pan until hot – you should feel the heat rising above it. Add the olive oil and swirl it around the pan. If the steaks have a thick layer of fat around the edge, hold them upright with a pair of tongs and fry the fat until golden brown and crisp. Turn them onto one side and fry for about 2–3 minutes, then repeat on the other side or until cooked to your liking. For medium rare steaks, the meat should feel slightly springy when pressed; medium steaks will feel slightly firmer. Transfer to a warm plate and leave to rest in a low oven or a warm spot in the kitchen, loosely covered with foil.

Add the shallot and garlic to the frying pan and fry for about 3–4 minutes until the shallot starts to soften. Pour in the cognac, stirring to deglaze, and scrape up any browned sediment on the bottom of the pan. Let bubble for 30 seconds, then stir in the green peppercorns, cream and mustard. Tip in any juices released from the resting steaks. Simmer for a few more minutes until the sauce lightly coats the back of a spoon. Taste and adjust the seasoning.

Place a sirloin steak on each warm plate and spoon over the green peppercorn sauce. Serve at once, with accompaniments of your choice.

SERVES 4

4 thick sirloin steaks, about 200–225g each
1 tbsp black peppercorns
sea salt
1½ tbsp olive oil
1 large shallot, peeled and finely chopped
1 garlic clove, peeled and finely crushed
splash of cognac or dry sherry
1 heaped tbsp green peppercorns in brine, rinsed and drained
200ml double cream
1 tbsp English mustard

Liver, bacon and caramelized onions

SERVES 4

1 large or 2 medium
   onions, peeled and
   thinly sliced
20g butter, plus an extra
   knob
1 tsp caster sugar
sea salt and black pepper
2 tsp sherry vinegar
600g calf's (or veal) liver
2 tbsp plain flour
1–2 tbsp olive oil
8 thin rashers of streaky
   bacon

It may not be everyone's favourite, but calf's liver can be meltingly tender and delicious when cooked properly. It also happens to be highly nutritious and low in fat. Serve with creamy mash or champ (see right) and wilted Savoy cabbage.

First, caramelize the onions. Melt the butter in a frying pan and add the onions, sugar and a pinch each of salt and pepper. Cook, stirring occasionally, over a medium heat for 10–12 minutes until the onions are soft and lightly caramelized. Add the sherry vinegar and let it bubble for 30 seconds until the onions are nicely glazed and golden brown. Remove the pan from the heat and keep warm.

Halve the calf's liver horizontally, removing any large membranes. Season the flour with salt and pepper and toss the liver in the flour to coat lightly and evenly all over. Set aside.

Heat a large frying pan until hot, then add the olive oil and fry the bacon for 3–4 minutes until browned and crisp all over. Remove to a plate lined with kitchen paper to drain off the excess oil.

Add a knob of butter to the pan and quickly fry the liver slices, in 2 or 3 batches, for 1–2 minutes on each side, depending on thickness. They should be browned on the outside, but still pink and succulent within.

Divide the liver between warm plates and top with the caramelized onions and crispy bacon rashers.

Pork chop with champ

It really pays to spend a little more on rare-breed pork from a reputable butcher. The full flavour of slow-to-mature pedigree pigs, such as Gloucester Old Spot, Middle White and Saddleback, is incomparable.

First, make the champ. Peel the potatoes and cut into even chunks. Add to a pan of cold salted water, bring to the boil and simmer for 10–15 minutes until tender when pierced with a knife. Drain well and push through a potato ricer into a bowl while still hot, or mash well.

Put the milk, butter and spring onions into the pan and simmer for 3–4 minutes until the onions are just soft. Pour over the potatoes and mix well, then stir in the crème fraîche and season with salt, pepper and a little lemon juice to taste. Return to the pan, ready to reheat to serve.

Trim off most of the fat from the chops, leaving a thin layer around the edge; set aside. Gently heat the olive oil in a wide frying pan over a medium-low heat. Add the sage leaves and fry for 30 seconds or until they begin to curl and crisp. Remove with a slotted spoon to a plate lined with kitchen paper. Add the garlic to the oil and sauté gently for 30–45 seconds until lightly golden. Remove to the plate, leaving the sage and garlic infused oil in the pan.

Increase the heat to medium. Season the pork chops on both sides and fry in the pan for about 3 minutes on each side until golden brown. Add a few knobs of butter to the pan along with the lemon juice. Swirl the pan to mix, then spoon the lemony pan juices over the pork and cook for a few more minutes until the pork is just firm when lightly pressed. Take off the heat.

Gently reheat the champ and pile onto warm plates. Top each serving with a pork chop, spoon over the pan juices and scatter over the crispy garlic and sage leaves to serve.

SERVES 4

4 good-quality pork
  chops, about 250g each,
  with bone
2 tbsp olive oil
8–10 large sage leaves
2 garlic cloves, peeled
  and thinly sliced
sea salt and black pepper
few knobs of butter
juice of 1 small lemon

CHAMP

1kg floury potatoes,
  such as King Edward
  or Maris Piper
300ml milk
30g butter
1 bunch of spring onions,
  about 6–8, trimmed
  and finely chopped
100ml crème fraîche
squeeze of lemon juice,
  to taste

WEEKEND ROASTS

Roast lamb with rosemary, garlic and anchovies

Crispy pork belly with roasted vegetables

Roast duck with orchard stuffing

Slow roast pork with apple and lavender sauce

Roast partridge with braised red cabbage

Roast chicken with gravy and bread sauce

Roast grouse with Madeira sauce

Christmas roast turkey infused with truffles

Roast saddle of venison with poached kumquats

Roast beef with red wine gravy

Roast lamb with rosemary, garlic and anchovies

SERVES 4–6

1.7kg boned shoulder of lamb

olive oil, to rub and drizzle

sea salt and black pepper

1 head of garlic

few rosemary sprigs

6–8 anchovies in oil, drained and halved

small handful of thyme sprigs

4 medium carrots, peeled, halved lengthways and cut into chunks

4 banana shallots (or 8–10 regular ones), peeled and halved lengthways

This is a lovely way to season a roast lamb. Rosemary and garlic impart a distinctive aroma, while the anchovies add a salty, savoury depth to the meat. Accompany with new potatoes or roast potatoes with rosemary (see page 247).

Preheat the oven to its highest setting. Place the lamb shoulder on a board and trim off any excess fat, leaving a thin, even layer. With the tip of a sharp knife, make slits all over the surface. Rub all over the meat with a little olive oil, and salt and pepper. Peel and thinly slice 2 garlic cloves. Insert a small sprig of rosemary, a slice of garlic and an anchovy half into each slit, using the tip of the knife to push them in.

Scatter the remaining garlic cloves (in their skins) and some thyme sprigs over the base of a roasting dish. Sprinkle over a little salt and pepper. Lay the lamb shoulder on top and surround with the carrots and shallots. Scatter over a few more thyme sprigs. Drizzle the lamb and vegetables with a little olive oil and sprinkle with salt and pepper.

Roast for 15 minutes until the meat begins to brown, then lower the oven setting to 180°C/Gas 4 and roast for another 30–40 minutes until the lamb is medium rare and pink in the middle. To check, insert a skewer into the thickest part and press gently – the juices should have a pinkish tinge. Remove from the oven, cover loosely with foil and allow to rest in a warm place for 15–20 minutes before carving.

Crispy pork belly with roasted vegetables

Roast pork belly is one of our Sunday lunch favourites. It's incredibly tasty and great value for money, especially when compared with other roasting joints. You don't even need to worry about basting the meat during roasting – its crispy fat layer does this for you. Accompany with roast potatoes (see page 247).

Preheat the oven to its highest setting. Pat the pork belly dry with kitchen paper, then score the rind at 5mm intervals using a sharp knife (or clean Stanley knife). Rub all over the rind and into the cuts with the caraway seeds and some salt and pepper.

Put the pork belly, skin side up, into a lightly oiled, large roasting tin and roast on the top shelf of the oven for 20–25 minutes until the skin starts to blister and crispen, then lower the oven setting to 170°C/Gas 3 and roast for a further hour.

Remove from the oven and spoon off most the rendered fat in the tin, leaving behind about 2 tbsp. Scatter the vegetables and thyme around the pork, toss them in the fat and sprinkle with salt and pepper. Return to the oven for another hour or until the vegetables and pork are tender when pierced with a knife.

If the crackling is not sufficiently crisp at the end of cooking, transfer the vegetables to a warm plate and place the pork under a hot grill until golden brown and crisp, but don't leave it unattended as the rind can easily catch. Cover the pork loosely with foil and leave to rest for 15 minutes in a warm place.

To serve, transfer the pork to a warm platter and arrange the roast vegetables around it.

SERVES 4–6

2kg pork belly with rind and ribs
1 tsp caraway seeds
sea salt and black pepper
olive oil, to oil the tin
2 medium turnips, cut into wedges (unpeeled)
4 banana shallots, halved lengthways (unpeeled)
1 large red onion, quartered (unpeeled)
150g baby fennel
150g Chantenay, or baby, carrots
few thyme sprigs

Roast duck with orchard stuffing

With its rich flavour and self-basting layer of fat, duck needs very little doing to it. The rendered fat is perfect for roasting potatoes and vegetables, or frying eggs, so don't discard it. To accompany our roast duck, we make a tasty stuffing with apples, onions and sausagemeat, cooking it separately.

Preheat the oven to 220°C/Gas 7. Trim off the large pieces of fat from the neck and cavity of the duck, then season the cavity. Lightly score the skin, taking care not to cut through the flesh, and rub all over with salt and pepper.

Place the duck in a roasting tin and roast for 15–20 minutes until it starts to brown, then lower the oven setting to 170°C/Gas 3 and roast for another 50–60 minutes, or until cooked to your liking. When you insert a skewer into the thickest part of the duck, the juices should run slightly pink for medium rare, or clear for well-done meat. If they are red, roast for another 15 minutes and check again.

While the duck is roasting, prepare the stuffing. Heat the olive oil in a pan and sweat the onion with some seasoning over a medium heat for 6–8 minutes until translucent and soft, stirring occasionally. Tip into a large bowl and leave to cool slightly.

Peel and grate the apples, discarding the core, and add to the onions with the sausagemeat and sage. Mix until well combined. To check the seasoning, fry off a little of the stuffing and taste, then adjust as necessary. Spread the mixture in a small casserole dish and cook on a lower oven shelf (beneath the duck) for 45–55 minutes or until cooked.

When cooked, transfer the duck to a warm platter, cover loosely with foil and leave to rest for 15–20 minutes. Skim off the fat from the pan juices, then add the wine and stock, and boil until reduced to a light gravy. Carve the duck into thin slices. Serve drizzled with the pan juices, garnished with watercress and accompanied by the stuffing.

SERVES 4

1 oven-ready duck, about
  2.3–2.5kg
sea salt and black pepper
splash of red wine
300ml chicken stock
  (see page 243)

ORCHARD STUFFING

1½ tbsp olive oil
1 large onion, peeled and
  chopped
3 eating apples, such as
  Braeburn or Cox
400g good-quality pork
  sausagemeat
4–6 sage leaves, finely
  chopped

TO GARNISH

handful of watercress
  sprigs

Slow roast pork
with apple and lavender sauce

SERVES 6–8

2kg boned shoulder
  of pork
sea salt and black pepper
3 medium onions, peeled
  and halved
4–5 bay leaves
olive oil, to oil the tin
200ml dry cider

**APPLE AND LAVENDER
SAUCE**

4 cooking apples
30g butter
30g caster sugar
few lavender stems (see
  above), flowers stripped

Slow cooking renders pork shoulder meltingly tender and the sauce balances the richness perfectly. If you don't have any lavender, replace the caster sugar with lavender sugar, which you can buy from selected supermarkets and delis.

Preheat the oven to its highest setting. Pat the pork rind dry with kitchen paper, then score at 5mm intervals. Rub all over with seasoning, massaging it into the cuts. Scatter the onion halves and bay leaves in a lightly oiled roasting tin and lay the pork on top, skin side up.

Roast for 20–25 minutes until the skin starts to blister and crispen, then lower the oven setting to 150°C/Gas 2. Spoon off most of the rendered fat in the tin. Pour the cider around the pork, cover with foil and roast for another 4–5 hours until very tender. Several times during roasting, lift the foil and baste the sides of the joint with the pan juices. The meat is ready when it can be easily shredded with a fork.

For the sauce, peel, core and roughly chop the apples. Melt the butter in a pan and add the apples with the sugar and lavender flowers. Cook over a medium-high heat for 10–15 minutes until soft and pulpy, stirring occasionally and adding a little water if needed. Sieve if preferred, and reheat gently before serving.

When cooked, take out the pork and turn the oven to its highest setting. Slice off the rind and place it on a baking sheet. Cover the pork shoulder loosely with foil and leave to rest in a warm place for 15–20 minutes. Meanwhile, roast the rind in the hot oven for 10–15 minutes until it turns to a crisp, golden crackling. Break into shards to serve.

Slice the pork shoulder thickly and serve with the pan juices, warm apple and lavender sauce and crispy crackling.

Roast partridge
with braised red cabbage

Partridge has an excellent mild flavour, which is ideal for those who prefer a less gamey taste. The braised red cabbage pairs well with any rich red meat or game, and it can be cooked in advance.

Preheat the oven to 180°C/Gas 4. For the braised cabbage, quarter, core and finely shred the red cabbage. Peel, core and grate the apple. Put the butter, sugar, vinegar and port into a large flameproof casserole dish and stir over a medium heat until the sugar has dissolved.

Add the bay leaves, star anise, cinnamon, ground cloves and a good pinch each of salt and pepper. Tip in the cabbage and apple and stir well. Bring to the boil, then cover with a lid (or foil) and transfer to the oven. Braise slowly for an hour, giving the cabbage a stir a few times. Remove the lid and cook, uncovered, for another 15–30 minutes until the cabbage is tender and the sauce is syrupy.

About 30 minutes before the cabbage will be ready to serve, season the partridges all over with salt and pepper. Heat the olive oil in a large frying pan and brown the partridges on all sides, turning occasionally, for about 1½ minutes on each side. Remove from the pan and place in a roasting tray.

Brush the butter over the birds, then drape the bacon rashers over the breasts. Roast in the oven for 18–20 minutes, or until the juices run clear when the thickest part of the thigh is pierced with a fine skewer.

Cover the birds with foil and leave to rest in a warm place for about 5–10 minutes before serving. Sprinkle the braised red cabbage with the chives and serve with the partridges.

SERVES 4

4 young partridges,
  about 300g each
sea salt and black pepper
2 tbsp olive oil
few knobs of butter,
  softened
4 thin smoked streaky
  bacon rashers

BRAISED RED CABBAGE

1 small red cabbage,
  about 600g
1 Braeburn apple
100g butter
150g dark brown sugar
75ml sherry vinegar or
  red wine vinegar
75ml port (or fruity
  red wine)
3 bay leaves
2 star anise
1 cinnamon stick
pinch of ground cloves
small handful of chives,
  finely chopped

Roast chicken with gravy and bread sauce

Roast chicken remains one of our nation's favourite Sunday lunches. For a change, instead of roasting a large chicken to feed four, try cooking two small chickens. This way, you can simply cut each chicken in half lengthways and serve each person their fair portion of white and dark meat.

First, make the bread sauce. Stud the onion halves with the cloves and put into a saucepan, along with the milk, bay leaf, thyme, peppercorns and a generous pinch of salt. Slowly bring to the boil, then remove from the heat and set aside to infuse for at least an hour.

Preheat the oven to 200°C/Gas 6. If the chickens are trussed, remove the strings and give the legs a gentle wiggle to loosen the joint slightly. Rub all over with salt and pepper and don't forget to season the cavities as well. Stuff the cavities with the onions, garlic, lemon halves and herbs. Put the chickens into a large roasting tin and drizzle with a little olive oil. Sprinkle a little salt and pepper over the surface.

Roast in the oven for 40–45 minutes until the skins are golden brown and crisp, and the chicken is just cooked through. To test, insert a thin skewer into the thickest part of the thigh – the juices should run clear. If they are at all pink, return to the oven for another 5–10 minutes and test again.

While the chickens are roasting, finish the bread sauce. Strain the milk into a clean saucepan, discarding the flavourings. Reheat gently, then stir in the breadcrumbs and butter. Simmer gently for a few minutes until the sauce thickens. We serve our bread sauce quite thick; if you prefer it thinner, thin with hot milk to the desired consistency. Season well to taste with salt and pepper and a generous grating of nutmeg. Transfer to a warm jug or bowl and keep warm.

(continued overleaf)

SERVES 4

2 small chickens, about
   1.3kg each
sea salt and black pepper
2 onions, peeled and
   quartered
1 head of garlic, halved
   horizontally
1 lemon, halved
small handful of thyme
2 bay leaves
olive oil, to drizzle
1 heaped tbsp plain flour
½ tsp tomato purée
splash of dry white wine
500ml chicken stock
   (see page 243)

BREAD SAUCE

1 onion, peeled and
   halved lengthways
5–6 cloves
600ml whole milk,
   or more to taste
1 bay leaf
few thyme sprigs
1 tsp black peppercorns
120g fresh white
   breadcrumbs
50g butter
freshly grated nutmeg

When the chickens are ready, lift them up and tip out the juices from the cavities into the roasting tin, then place on a warm platter. Put the lemon halves to one side, but discard the vegetables and herbs from the cavities. Cover the chickens loosely with foil and leave to rest in a warm spot.

Skim off most of the fat from the roasting tin, leaving behind about 1½–2 tbsp. Put the tin on the hob and stir in the flour and tomato purée. Cook, stirring, over a medium-high heat for a couple of minutes until the flour starts to colour. Add the wine and stir until smooth. Pour in the stock, stir well and bring to the boil. Let bubble until thickened to a gravy consistency. Taste and adjust the seasoning, adding a squeeze of juice from the roasted lemons, if you wish. Strain the gravy through a fine sieve into a warm jug.

Carve the chickens or simply halve them and serve with the gravy, bread sauce and seasonal vegetables of your choice.

Roast grouse with
Madeira sauce

When grouse is in season, from mid-August through to early December, it is a delicious option for the Sunday roast. The Madeira sauce also works well with chicken.

Preheat the oven to 200°C/Gas 6. Rub all over each bird with salt and pepper. Heat the olive oil in a wide frying pan and brown the birds all over for about 5 minutes. Transfer to a lightly oiled, large roasting tin, breast upwards. Brush with 30g butter and season again. Drape the bacon over the breasts and roast for 15–20 minutes until the juices run clear when a skewer is inserted into the thickest part of the thigh.

While the grouse is cooking, make the sauce. Melt the butter in a saucepan and brown the bacon, with the grouse giblets (except the heart and liver) if using, and a little seasoning. Stir in the onion and sweat over a medium heat for 4–6 minutes to soften. Increase the heat, add the herbs and pour in the Madeira. Let bubble until reduced by two-thirds. Add the stock and boil again until reduced by two-thirds and slightly thickened. Season to taste. Strain the sauce into a clean pan.

When cooked, loosely cover the grouse with foil and leave to rest in a warm place for 5–10 minutes. If you have them, season the hearts and livers and fry them in the hot frying pan with a knob of butter for 1–2 minutes each side. Transfer to a food processor and blend to a smooth paste, seasoning well to taste.

Toast the bread slices, remove the crusts and cut into triangles. Spread with the paste if you've made it, otherwise leave plain, and place the toasts on warm plates. Reheat the Madeira sauce. Place a grouse on each plate and garnish with watercress. Serve with the Madeira sauce, bread sauce if wished, and buttery Savoy cabbage.

SERVES 4

4 young grouse, about 350g each (giblets reserved if available)
sea salt and black pepper
2 tbsp olive oil
30–40g butter, softened
8 thin, unsmoked streaky bacon rashers

MADEIRA SAUCE

20g butter
2 unsmoked streaky bacon rashers, derinded and chopped
1 small onion, peeled and finely chopped
few rosemary sprigs, leaves stripped
few thyme sprigs, leaves stripped
300ml Madeira
750ml chicken stock (see page 243)

TO SERVE

4 slices of white bread, toasted
1 bunch of watercress, stalks trimmed
bread sauce (optional), see page 201

Christmas roast turkey infused with truffles

SERVES 8–10

1 oven-ready turkey,
  about 5kg, with giblets,
  at room temperature
250g unsalted butter,
  softened
2 tsp truffle paste
  (or 1–2 grated fresh
  black truffles)
sea salt and black pepper
1 lemon, halved
1 orange, halved
1 large onion, peeled and
  halved
1 head of garlic, halved
  horizontally
2 bay leaves
small handful of thyme
  sprigs

MUSHROOM STUFFING

3 tbsp olive oil, plus extra
  to drizzle
500g chestnut
  mushrooms, trimmed
  and chopped
2 large onions, peeled
  and finely chopped
2 celery sticks, finely
  chopped
4 smoked bacon rashers,
  derinded and chopped

Few things are more festive than a traditional roast turkey. To ensure a moist, succulent bird, we stuff lots of butter between the skin and breast meat, flavouring the butter with fresh black truffles or truffle paste for a treat.

Preheat the oven to 220°C/Gas 7. Pat the the turkey dry inside and out with kitchen paper. Mash the butter in a bowl and beat in the truffle paste (or truffles) with some seasoning. Spoon into a piping bag fitted with a 1cm plain nozzle. Working from the neck end, use your fingers to carefully loosen the skin covering the breasts and thighs, then pipe the truffle butter underneath. Massage the skin to spread the butter evenly.

Season the cavity with salt and pepper, then stuff with the lemon, orange, onion, garlic and herbs. Spread any remaining butter over the breast and season well. Put the turkey into a lightly oiled roasting tin and roast for 15 minutes, then lower the oven setting to 180°C/Gas 4. Roast for a further 1¾–2¼ hours, basting every half-hour with the pan juices. (Timing will vary according to the size and shape of the bird, so check for doneness after 1¾ hours.)

While the turkey is roasting, make the stuffing. Heat 2 tbsp olive oil in a wide frying pan and fry the mushrooms over a high heat until golden brown and most of the moisture released has cooked off, then tip into a bowl. Heat the remaining oil in the pan and fry the onions, celery and bacon for 6–8 minutes to soften and colour. Add to the mushrooms with the breadcrumbs, stock and herbs. Finally, stir in the beaten eggs.

Either shape the stuffing into golf-ball-sized balls with floured hands and place on an oiled roasting tray, or loosely pack into a 900g loaf tin. Drizzle lightly with oil before baking, allowing 20–30 minutes for stuffing balls, or 35–45 minutes for a loaf tin.

Start off the gravy while the turkey is in the oven. Heat the olive oil in a wide pan and fry the giblets with seasoning until browned all over. Add the vegetables with the herbs and sauté for 6–8 minutes to soften. Pour in the stock and simmer over a low heat for about an hour. Strain through a fine sieve and set aside.

To check if the turkey is ready, pierce the thickest part of each thigh with a metal skewer and press lightly. The juices should run clear or a pale golden colour; if they have a pinkish tinge, return to the oven for another 15–20 minutes and check again. When ready, transfer the turkey to a warm platter, cover with foil and rest in a warm place for 30 minutes before carving.

Pour the juices from the roasting tin into a heatproof jug and leave for a few minutes until the fat separates on the surface. Add 1–2 tbsp of it back to the roasting pan, then pour off the rest of the fat. Mix the turkey juices with the stock and set aside.

Put the turkey roasting tin on the hob over a medium heat. Add the flour and stir for a few minutes, then pour in the stock and stir well. Let bubble until thickened to the desired consistency. Taste and adjust the seasoning, then pour into a warmed gravy boat to serve with the turkey.

200g breadcrumbs
50ml chicken stock
 (see page 243)
small handful of sage
 leaves, chopped
handful of parsley
 leaves, chopped
2 medium eggs

GIBLET GRAVY
1½ tbsp olive oil
1 large onion, peeled and
 chopped
1 large carrot, peeled and
 chopped
2 celery sticks, trimmed
 and chopped
1 bay leaf
few thyme sprigs
1 litre chicken stock
 (see page 243)
2 tbsp plain flour

Roast saddle of venison
with poached kumquats

Lightly spiced, poached kumquats add an exotic twist to roast venison. We like to roast the saddle on the bone for extra flavour. Ask your butcher to remove the rib bones but leave on the central backbone to keep the two loins together. As venison is a lean meat, it helps to tie a thin layer of fat on top of the saddle to protect and baste the meat as it roasts.

Preheat the oven to 200°C/Gas 6. Rub all over the venison with salt and pepper, then place in a lightly oiled roasting tin. Drizzle over a little olive oil and sprinkle with a little more salt and pepper. Roast for about 50–60 minutes until golden brown all over, and the meat is medium rare and pink in the middle. To check if the venison is ready, insert a skewer into the thickest part of the roast and press lightly – the juices should have a pinkish tinge.

Prepare the kumquats when you've put the venison into the oven. Put the sugar, water, thyme, star anise and peppercorns into a small saucepan and heat gently, stirring to dissolve the sugar, then simmer for about 10 minutes to reduce the syrup and thicken it slightly. In the meantime, halve the kumquats and remove the pips with the tip of a knife. Add the kumquats to the syrup, bring back to a simmer and poach for 20–30 minutes until soft and the syrup has thickened. Remove from the heat and leave to cool completely.

When the venison is ready, cover loosely with foil and leave to rest in a warm place for about 20 minutes. Carve the saddle into thick slices, following along the curve of the central bone. Sprinkle the slices with a little salt and pepper and serve them on a warm platter with the poached kumquats. Braised chicory and roasted or mashed parsnips are lovely accompaniments.

SERVES 8

2.7kg saddle of venison
  with bone
sea salt and black pepper
olive oil, to drizzle

POACHED KUMQUATS

125g caster sugar
200ml water
few thyme sprigs
2 star anise
5–6 black peppercorns,
  lightly crushed
300g kumquats
2 tbsp apricot jam

Roast beef with red wine gravy

SERVES 4–6

1.2kg joint of beef sirloin
  or rib-eye
2½ tbsp plain flour
½ tsp celery salt
½ tsp freshly ground
  black pepper
olive oil, to drizzle
1 tbsp English mustard
1 large red onion, peeled
  and cut into wedges
1 medium carrot, peeled
  and cut into chunks
2 celery sticks, peeled
  and cut into chunks
few thyme sprigs
few rosemary sprigs
2 bay leaves
300ml red wine
600ml beef or veal stock
  (see page 244)

TO SERVE

Yorkshire puddings
  (see page 248)

A beautifully browned joint of beef from the oven is always a welcome sight. It is important to start off with a good-quality joint, and to finish off by resting the beef. This lets the juices redistribute and ensures succulent meat.

Preheat the oven to 230°C/Gas 8. Trim off any excess fat from the beef, leaving on a thin, even layer. Mix 1 tbsp flour with the celery salt and pepper in a small bowl. Drizzle a little olive oil all over the beef, then rub with a little salt and pepper. Brush the fat with the mustard, then coat with the seasoned flour.

Put the onion, carrot, celery and herbs into a lightly oiled roasting tin. Season and drizzle with a little olive oil. Place the beef on top and drizzle with a little more olive oil. Roast in the oven for 15 minutes, then lower the oven setting to 190°C/Gas 5 and roast for another 35–45 minutes for medium rare meat. To check, insert a skewer into the meat and press lightly – the redder the juice, the rarer the meat. Transfer to a warm platter, cover loosely with foil and rest in a warm spot for 20 minutes.

While the beef is resting, make the gravy. Transfer the vegetables and herbs in the roasting tin to a saucepan. Pour off all but 1–1½ tbsp oil from the roasting tin and place the tin over a medium heat. Stir in the remaining 1½ tbsp flour and cook, stirring, for a couple of minutes, then pour in the wine. Bring to a simmer, scraping up any sediment from the bottom of the tin. Tip into the saucepan and bring to the boil. Let bubble until the wine has reduced by half. Pour in the stock and again boil until reduced by half, or to a light gravy consistency. Season well to taste. Strain through a fine sieve into a warm jug, pressing down on the vegetables to extract the juices.

Carve the beef into thin slices and serve with the gravy, Yorkshire puddings, roast potatoes and other accompaniments of your choice.

PUDDINGS

Clementine cakes with cranberry sauce

Hot chocolate fondants

Plum fool

Treacle tart

Rice pudding with poached rhubarb and ginger

Summer pudding

Jam roly poly

Manchester tart

Apple charlotte

Pimm's jellies

Sussex pond pudding

London syllabub

Sherry trifle

Gypsy tart

Queen of puddings

Pears poached in perry

Strawberry tart

Clementine cakes with cranberry sauce

These clementine-topped upside down cakes are best eaten warm from the oven. Keep any extra cranberry sauce in the fridge to spoon over pancakes and waffles, or pair with ham.

Preheat the oven to 180°C/Gas 4. Butter 6 or 7 small pudding moulds or ramekins, depending on size. Heat a wide pan over a high heat. Toss the clementine segments with 50g sugar. Tip into the pan, add 1 tbsp water and cook for a minute until slightly softened but still holding their shape. Spoon them into the base of the prepared moulds, along with the juices. Set aside to cool while making the sponge.

Cream the butter and remaining 125g caster sugar together in a bowl until light and fluffy. Gradually beat in the eggs, one at a time, adding 1 tbsp of the flour with the second egg. Beat in the vanilla extract and orange zest. Fold in the rest of the flour in two batches. Finally fold through the orange juice until evenly combined.

Spoon the mixture into the moulds to two-thirds fill them, and smooth the tops. Stand on a baking tray and bake for 20–25 minutes or until risen and golden brown on top. To test, insert a thin skewer inserted into the centre – it should come out clean.

While the cakes are in the oven, make the cranberry sauce. Put the cranberries, sugar, clementine juice and a splash of water into a wide pan and stir frequently over a high heat until the berries have burst and softened. Keep cooking for 10 minutes or so, until the mixture is thick and pulpy. Transfer to a bowl to cool.

Once the clementine cakes are cooked, leave them in their moulds for a few minutes, then run a thin, flexible knife around the edge of each one and invert onto a serving plate. Serve warm, with a spoonful of cranberry sauce on the side and a generous drizzle of cream.

MAKES 6–7

125g unsalted butter, plus extra to grease
6 large, ripe clementines, peeled and segmented
175g caster sugar
1 tbsp water
2 large eggs
125g self-raising flour, sifted
1 tsp vanilla extract
finely grated zest of 1 orange
2 tbsp orange juice

CRANBERRY SAUCE

300g cranberries (thawed, if frozen)
150g caster sugar
juice of 3 clementines

TO SERVE

pouring cream

Hot chocolate fondants

SERVES 6

90g unsalted butter, softened, plus extra to grease

100g dark chocolate, roughly chopped

2 large eggs

2 large egg yolks

50g caster sugar

20g plain flour

TO SERVE

good-quality vanilla ice cream

This is the ultimate pudding for chocolate lovers. It has the consistency of a moist chocolate cake on the outside and a warm and gooey mousse in the middle. The puddings must be eaten straight after baking, preferably with vanilla ice cream.

Preheat the oven to 180°C/Gas 4. Butter 6 small ramekins or pudding moulds and stand them on a baking tray.

Put the butter and chocolate into a heatproof bowl and set it over a pan of gently simmering water. Stir frequently until the butter and chocolate have melted and the mixture is smooth. Remove the bowl from the pan and leave to cool.

Meanwhile, whisk the eggs, egg yolks and sugar together in a large bowl using an electric beater. Keep whisking until the mixture is pale, thick and has roughly tripled in volume. Carefully fold in the chocolate mixture, followed by the flour. Spoon the mixture into the buttered ramekins, dividing it equally. (The puddings can be prepared a day ahead to this stage and kept in the fridge.)

Bake the chocolate fondants just before serving, allowing 7–8 minutes (or if taking them straight from the fridge, bake for 10–11 minutes). They should be set on the outside, but the centre should be soft and slightly runny.

To unmould, run a thin, flexible knife around each pudding and invert it onto a serving plate. Serve at once, with vanilla ice cream.

Plum fool

This simple British classic is a great way to use up ripe plums in the autumn. Any variety of plum will work for this recipe but do taste a little first for sweetness, then adjust the amount of sugar accordingly.

Cut the plums in half, remove the stones and roughly chop the fruit. Place in a saucepan with the sugar, lemon juice and water, and slowly bring to a simmer. Cook gently for 10–15 minutes until soft. Transfer the plums and syrup to a blender and blend to a smooth purée. Tip into a wide bowl and leave to cool completely.

Whip the double cream and icing sugar to soft peaks. Fold through the crème fraîche, then add two-thirds of the puréed plums and give the mixture a few folds to create a rippled effect.

Divide the remaining plum purée between serving glasses and top with the cream mixture. Serve immediately or chill until required

SERVES 6–7

400g firm, but ripe plums
100g caster sugar, or to taste
juice of 1 lemon
3 tbsp water
300ml double cream
1–2 tbsp icing sugar, to taste
300ml crème fraîche, or thick creamy yoghurt

Treacle tart

SERVES 8

300g sweet flan pastry
  (see page 248)

450g golden syrup
85g white breadcrumbs
finely grated zest and
  juice of 1 lemon
½ tsp ground ginger
60g butter, melted
3 large egg yolks
70ml double cream
½ tsp black treacle

TO SERVE

whipped cream or crème
  fraîche

This is the treacle tart to die for. It tastes even better a day after baking, when the breadcrumbs have had time to absorb the wonderfully moist filling. Serve individual slices with dollops of whipped cream or crème fraîche to tone down the sweetness of the filling.

Roll out the pastry on a lightly floured surface to a large round, the thickness of a £1 coin. Use to line a 23–24cm round shallow tart tin, with removable base, leaving some excess pastry overhanging the rim. Leave to rest in the fridge for 30 minutes. Meanwhile, preheat the oven to 190°C/Gas 5.

Line the pastry case with baking paper and dried or ceramic baking beans and bake 'blind' for 15–20 minutes until the sides are set and lightly golden. Remove the paper and beans and return to the oven for another 5 minutes or until the base is cooked through. While still warm, cut off the excess pastry to level with the rim of the tin. Lower the oven setting to 140°C/Gas 1.

For the filling, gently heat the golden syrup by immersing the bottle or tin in a bowl of hot water for a few minutes. Mix the breadcrumbs, lemon zest and ground ginger together in a large bowl and make a well in the middle. Pour in the warm golden syrup and add the butter, egg yolks, cream, treacle and lemon juice. Stir well to mix.

Pour the filling into the pastry case. Bake for 30–40 minutes until the top has just set, but the centre is slightly wobbly when you shake the tin gently. It should still feel slightly soft in the centre. Let the tart cool completely before slicing and serving, with cream or crème fraîche.

Rice pudding with
poached rhubarb and ginger

A warming rice pudding is truly comforting when there is a chill in the air. We usually serve rice pudding warm, but there is no reason why you can't enjoy it cold – just stir a little extra cream into the cold pudding to loosen it, as it tends to firm up in the fridge. The rhubarb should be chilled in its poaching syrup so that the flavours continue to meld together.

First, make the rice pudding. Put the rice, milk, salt and sugar into a heavy-based saucepan. Bring to the boil, stirring once or twice, then turn the heat down to its lowest setting and partially cover the pan with a lid. Simmer slowly for about 40–50 minutes until the rice is tender, giving it a stir every once in a while to prevent it from catching and burning on the bottom of the pan. You may also want to top up with a little more hot milk or boiling water halfway through cooking if the rice appears to be a bit dry.

For the rhubarb, put the sugar, water and stem ginger into a medium saucepan and stir over a low heat until the sugar has dissolved. Increase the heat slightly and simmer for a few minutes. Meanwhile, trim the rhubarb and cut diagonally into short lengths. Add to the pan and poach for 3–4 minutes until the pieces are slightly softened but still holding their shape.

Drain the poached rhubarb and place in a bowl, reserving the syrup. Pour the syrup back into the pan and boil vigorously until reduced and thickened. Pour over the rhubarb pieces and leave to cool slightly.

When the rice pudding is ready, remove the pan from the heat and leave to stand for 5 minutes, then stir in the cream, if using. Spoon into individual bowls and top with the poached rhubarb to serve.

SERVES 4

RICE PUDDING
200g pudding rice
600ml whole milk
pinch of fine sea salt
100g caster sugar
200ml single cream
 (optional)

POACHED RHUBARB
125g caster sugar
450ml water
1 ball of stem ginger in
 syrup, finely sliced into
 matchsticks
300g rhubarb

Summer pudding

SERVES 6

400g strawberries, hulled

900g mixed berries, such as blackberries, blueberries, raspberries and redcurrants

170g caster sugar

5 tbsp crème de cassis (or kirsch)

3 tbsp water

1 brioche loaf (unsliced)

TO SERVE

lightly whipped cream

Along with strawberries and cream, summer pudding is the quintessential British summer dessert. Use any combination of ripe, soft berries, but do try to get a mix of red and dark berries.

Halve the strawberries, or quarter them if large. Strip the redcurrants from their stalks. Set aside with the rest of the berries.

Put the sugar, cassis and water into a saucepan and stir over a low heat to dissolve the sugar, then simmer for 5–8 minutes to reduce the syrup slightly. Tip in the blackberries and redcurrants and cook for a minute. Add the rest of the berries and simmer for a couple of minutes until softened slightly, but still holding their shape. Tip them into a sieve set over a large bowl to catch the juice. Let cool slightly.

Have ready a 1.2 litre pudding basin. Cut off the crusts from the brioche, then cut lengthways into thin slices, about 5mm thick. Cut out a brioche round the size of the base of the pudding basin, using a pastry cutter. Dip in the juice, then place in the basin. Set aside a large slice for the top. Line the side of the basin with the rest of the brioche slices, dipping them in the juice first and overlapping them slightly; trim to fit as necessary.

Pile the warm fruit into the brioche-lined basin. Cut a lid from the reserved brioche slice, dip in the fruit juice and lay over the berries. (If necessary, use the brioche trimmings to fill in any gaps.) Spoon over 2–3 tbsp juice, saving the rest for serving.

Cover with cling film, then press a saucer on top of the pudding and weigh down with a tin. Chill for a few hours or overnight.

When ready to serve, uncover, then run a thin, flexible knife around the side of the pudding. Turn out onto a serving dish and spoon over the reserved juice. Slice and serve with lightly whipped cream.

Jam roly poly

SERVES 4–6
250g self-raising flour
pinch of fine sea salt
70g shredded suet
50g unsalted butter,
  melted
about 125ml whole milk
3–4 tbsp raspberry jam,
  warmed
1 medium egg, beaten
  with 1 tbsp milk,
  to glaze
caster sugar, to sprinkle

TO SERVE
custard (see page 249)

This old-time favourite is enjoying something of a revival on traditional pub menus. It is delightfully simple to make and is likely to be popular with children. For grown-ups, serve it with dollops of crème fraîche flavoured with Grand Marnier or Cointreau.

Preheat the oven to 190°C/Gas 5. Sift the flour and salt together into a bowl. Add the suet, mix well, then make a well in the middle. Add the melted butter, then pour in most of the milk, holding back 1–2 tbsp. Mix to a soft but not sticky dough, adding the remaining milk as necessary if the dough is too dry.

Roughly shape the dough into a rectangle and roll it out on a lightly floured surface to a 5mm thickness. Trim the edges to neaten. Spread a thin layer of jam over the dough, leaving a 1.5cm margin clear around the edges. Dab the margin with a little water or milk. Roll up the rectangle from a long side to form a neat log and lift onto a baking sheet, placing it seam side down.

Brush the log with the egg glaze and sprinkle with caster sugar. Bake for about 35–40 minutes until the top is lightly golden. Don't worry if the roly poly has cracked in the middle – this is a characteristic of the pudding. Leave to cool for a few minutes before slicing and serving, with warm custard.

Manchester tart

This is a deliciously simple old-fashioned jam and custard tart with the addition of sliced bananas and desiccated coconut. Purists may argue that the original recipe does not include bananas, but we love the way they bring the flavours of the jam and custard together. You can leave them out if you prefer.

Roll out the pastry on a lightly floured surface to a large round, the thickness of a £1 coin. Use to line a 20cm round tart tin, 2–2.5cm deep, with removable base, leaving some excess pastry overhanging the rim. Leave to rest in the fridge for 30 minutes. Meanwhile, preheat the oven to 190°C/Gas 5.

Line the pastry case with baking paper and dried or ceramic baking beans and bake 'blind' for 15–20 minutes until the sides are set and lightly golden. Remove the paper and beans and return to the oven for another 5 minutes. While still warm, cut off the excess pastry to level with the rim of the tin. Leave to cool completely.

Whip the cream and icing sugar together in a bowl until just stiff, then fold through the pastry cream until well combined. Spread the jam over the base of the pastry case. Peel and thinly slice the bananas, and toss with the lemon juice in a bowl. Arrange the banana slices in a single layer over the jam, then spread the pastry cream mixture on top. (You may have a little over – enjoy it as a cook's treat).

Lightly toast the desiccated coconut in a dry pan, tossing frequently, until lightly golden brown and fragrant. Tip into a bowl and mix with the caster sugar, then sprinkle over the top of the tart. Serve at room temperature or chilled.

SERVES 4–6

300g sweet flan pastry
 (see page 248)
75ml double cream
1 tbsp icing sugar
1 quantity (650ml)
 pastry cream
 (see page 249)
3 tbsp raspberry jam
2 ripe medium bananas
squeeze of lemon juice
1½ tbsp desiccated
 coconut
1½ tbsp caster sugar

Apple charlotte

SERVES 6–8

800g mixture of
 Bramley and eating
 apples, such as
 Braeburn or Cox
2 tbsp golden caster
 sugar
½ tsp ground cinnamon
120g unsalted butter
3 tbsp raisins or sultanas
2 tsp honey
juice of ½ lemon
1 loaf of one- or two-day
 old white bread
 (unsliced)
icing sugar, to dust

TO SERVE

softly whipped cream or
 custard (see page 249)

A traditional charlotte is a great way to make a tempting pudding from stale bread and apples. Usually the filling consists solely of Bramley apples, cooked to a purée, but we like to include some eating apples, which retain their shape better and lend an interesting texture to the filling.

Peel, core and thinly slice the apples, then toss with the sugar and cinnamon. Melt 20g butter in a heavy-based (preferably non-stick) frying pan. Toss the apples in the melted butter to coat, then add the raisins, honey and lemon juice. Cook over a high heat for 5–6 minutes until the sugar has dissolved and the liquid has cooked off. The apple filling must be fairly dry, otherwise it will make the pudding soggy. Remove from the heat and leave to cool.

Preheat the oven to 200°C/Gas 6. Melt the remaining butter and use some to brush a 20cm round shallow cake tin, with removable base. Cut off the crusts, then thinly slice the bread. Lightly roll over each slice with a rolling pin to flatten slightly and brush both sides with butter. Line the base and side of the tin with the bread slices, overlapping them slightly, and letting them extend above the rim.

Fill the bread-lined tin with the cooled apple mixture, using a slotted spoon to leave behind any excess liquid. Fold over the extending bread slices and fill the middle and any gaps with more buttered slices. Brush the top with butter. Lightly press a similar sized plate on top to ensure that the apple filling is tightly packed, then remove it. Bake the pudding for 20 minutes. Lightly dust the top with icing sugar and bake for another 10–15 minutes until the sugar has lightly caramelized.

Let the apple charlotte stand for a few minutes before unmoulding onto a large plate. Slice and serve while still warm, with softly whipped cream or warm custard, if you prefer.

Pimm's jellies

These mouth-watering jellies are as refreshing as the cocktail itself. They make a pretty dessert for a dinner party, or you can simply enjoy them as a cool, teatime treat.

Put the sugar, water and lemon juice into a saucepan over a low heat to dissolve the sugar, giving the mixture an occasional stir. Leave to simmer for about 5 minutes. Meanwhile, soak the gelatine leaves in a shallow dish of cold water for about 5 minutes until softened.

Take the pan off the heat. Squeeze out the excess water from the gelatine leaves, then add them to the hot syrup and stir well to dissolve. Pour into a large bowl and allow to cool slightly, stirring occasionally, before adding the Pimm's and lemonade.

Now cool the jelly quickly: set the bowl over a larger bowl one-third filled with iced water. Stir the jelly mixture frequently as the mixture cools. When it is beginning to set, lift the bowl off the ice bath. Fold the mint leaves and strawberries through the jelly to disperse them evenly. (If you add them earlier, they will simply float to the surface.)

Divide the jelly mixture between individual pudding moulds or serving glasses. Chill for a few hours, or overnight, until set.

To unmould, briefly dip a jelly mould into a bowl of warm water, then invert on to a serving plate. Holding the mould and plate together firmly, give them a few shakes to release the jelly. Serve with a jug of pouring cream on the side.

NOTE: If using a different brand of leaf gelatine, you may need to adjust the quantity of leaves; refer to the packet instructions for setting capacity.

SERVES 4–5

100g caster sugar
100ml water
juice of ½ lemon
7 Supercook gelatine
  leaves (see note)
175ml Pimm's No. 1
500ml sparkling
  lemonade
few mint sprigs, leaves
  torn
400g strawberries,
  hulled and quartered

TO SERVE
pouring cream

Sussex pond pudding

SUET PASTRY
softened butter, to brush
100g self-raising flour
50g fresh white
  breadcrumbs
finely grated zest of
  1 lemon
75g vegetable suet
5–6 tbsp whole milk

LEMON FILLING
100g unsalted butter,
  diced
100g light brown or
  Demerara sugar
2 lemons

TO SERVE
good-quality vanilla
  ice cream

For this inventive, classic pudding, whole or half lemons are encased with butter and sugar in suet pastry and steamed until soft. As you cut into the pudding, the sweet buttery lemony juices flood the plate to form a pond.

Brush four small pudding moulds with butter; set aside. Sift the flour into a large bowl and mix in the breadcrumbs, lemon zest and suet. Make a well in the middle and add 5 tbsp milk. Mix to a smooth dough that comes away from the side of the bowl. If the dough seems too dry, add a little extra milk.

Roll the dough out on a lightly floured surface and divide into four portions. From each portion, cut out a quarter of the dough for the lid and roll out the larger piece to a round big enough to line a pudding mould. Neatly line the moulds with the pastry rounds, pressing down on the base and sides to even out the thickness.

For the filling, divide the butter and brown sugar equally between the moulds. Trim off the pointed ends of the lemons, then cut in half and remove any pips. Put a lemon half into each mould. Roll out the other pieces of dough for the lids. Dampen the edges with a little water, lay the lids over the filling and press the pastry edges together to seal. Cover the puddings with pieces of pleated foil and tie in place with kitchen string. (Make a string handle so that they can be lifted easily.)

Bring a 2–3cm depth of water to the boil in a large saucepan (that will take all the moulds). Lower them into the water, which should come two-thirds of the way up their sides. Put the lid on the pan and steam for about 2 hours, topping up with boiling water as necessary.

Serve the puddings while still warm. Remove the foil, run a small knife around the sides and invert the puddings onto warm, lipped plates. Serve immediately, with generous scoops of vanilla ice cream.

London syllabub

SERVES 4–6

300ml sherry or Madeira
4–4½ tbsp icing sugar,
  to taste
pinch of freshly grated
  nutmeg
570ml double cream

TO SERVE

4–6 sponge fingers or
  shortbreads

Originating from the Elizabethan era, a London syllabub is one of the easiest desserts you can make. Comprising sherry or Madeira wine flavoured with a hint of nutmeg and topped with sweetened whipped cream, it is simple and satisfying. Assemble the syllabub in small glasses to show off the distinct layers.

Stir the sherry, 1 tbsp icing sugar and a pinch of nutmeg together in a bowl until the sugar has dissolved. Taste for sweetness, adding a little more sugar if you wish. Divide evenly between small serving glasses.

Softly whip the cream with the remaining icing sugar until just stiff, taking care not to over-whisk. Top each glass with a few generous spoonfuls of whipped cream, then chill in the fridge for at least an hour or overnight before serving, with sponge fingers or shortbreads for dipping.

Sherry trifle

SERVES 8–10

1 good-quality ready-
made jam-filled
Swiss roll

2–3 tbsp sweet sherry,
to taste

350g jar pitted morello
cherries in syrup,
drained

300ml double cream,
softly whipped

1 tbsp icing sugar

50g toasted pistachios,
roughly chopped

CUSTARD

200ml double cream

400ml whole milk

80g caster sugar

1 vanilla pod

6 large egg yolks

4 tsp cornflour

A well-made sherry trifle is a guaranteed crowd pleaser. This is an easy version and we've added some chopped pistachios to give the trifle some crunch and a varied texture. To make it child-friendly, you can leave out the sherry and replace the nuts with crushed amaretti or gingernut biscuits if you like.

First, make the custard. Put the cream, milk and 1 tbsp sugar into a heavy-based saucepan and bring to a simmer. Split the vanilla pod lengthways and scrape out the seeds into a large bowl (see note). Add the egg yolks, remaining sugar and cornflour, and whisk until pale and creamy. Gradually whisk the hot creamy milk into the yolk mixture. Rinse out the pan and wipe dry.

Strain the mixture back into the pan and stir over a low heat with a wooden spoon until it thickens enough to heavily coat the back of the spoon. Take care not to overheat or it may curdle. Pour the custard into a bowl and allow to cool, stirring every so often to stop a skin forming.

To assemble the trifle, cut the Swiss roll into 1–1.5cm slices and arrange them over the base and a little way up the side of a large glass serving bowl. Sprinkle with the sherry, then layer most of the cherries on top, reserving the rest. Pile the cooled custard over the cherries.

Whip the cream and icing sugar together in a bowl to soft peaks, then spoon over the custard. (The trifle can be prepared ahead to this stage, covered and kept chilled for up to 2 days.)

Just before serving, arrange the remaining cherries on top of the trifle and sprinkle over the chopped pistachios.

NOTE: Don't discard the vanilla pod once you've taken out the seeds. Submerge it in a jar of caster sugar to make vanilla sugar.

Gypsy tart

With its light, moussey, sugar-rich filling, this tart is sure to please all those with a sweet tooth. Serve each slice with a dollop of crème fraîche, or tart soft fruit, to counteract the sweetness of the filling.

Roll out the pastry on a lightly floured surface to a large round, the thickness of a £1 coin. Use to line a 23–24cm round tart tin, 2–2.5cm deep, with removable base, leaving some excess pastry overhanging the rim. Rest in the fridge for 30 minutes. Melt the chocolate in a bowl set over a pan of hot water, then take off the heat and cool slightly.

Preheat the oven to 190°C/Gas 5. Line the pastry with baking paper and dried or ceramic baking beans and bake 'blind' for 15–20 minutes until the sides are set and lightly golden. Remove the paper and beans and return to the oven for another 5 minutes. While still warm, cut off the excess pastry to level with the rim of the tin. Brush the base and sides with the melted chocolate and leave to cool and set. Turn the oven up to 200°C/Gas 6.

For the filling, whisk the evaporated milk and sugar together, ideally using a free-standing electric mixer, to dissolve the sugar. Keep whisking until the mixture has thickened to a frothy, light consistency, the colour of a cappuccino. This may take as long as 15–20 minutes.

Pour the filling into the pastry case until it almost reaches the top. Carefully place in the oven and bake for 10–15 minutes until the filling is set on the surface, but the middle is slightly wobbly when you gently shake the tin. Leave the tart to cool completely, during which time it will continue to set.

Once cooled, carefully unmould the tart, slice and serve as a dessert, with crème fraîche if you like, or as a sweet treat with a cup of coffee or tea.

SERVES 8

300g shortcrust pastry (see page 248)
30g white chocolate, chopped
2 x 170g tins evaporated milk
250g dark muscovado sugar

TO SERVE

crème fraîche (optional)

Queen of puddings

SERVES 6–8

150g brioche (or white
  bread)

150g caster sugar,
  plus 3 tbsp

finely grated zest of
  1 lemon, plus a squeeze
  of juice

600ml milk

50g unsalted butter,
  plus extra to grease

4 medium eggs,
  separated

3 tbsp strawberry or
  raspberry jam

This traditional English pudding is surprisingly light. Breadcrumbs – or in our case, buttery brioche crumbs – are baked in a custard mixture, then spread with jam and finished with a meringue 'crown'.

Cut off the crusts, then cut or tear the brioche into smaller pieces. Whiz to fine crumbs in a food processor. Tip into a bowl and mix with 3 tbsp sugar and the lemon zest. Heat the milk and butter gently in a saucepan until the butter has melted, then pour over the crumb mixture and leave to soak for 5–10 minutes.

Preheat the oven to 180°C/Gas 4 and butter a wide 1.5–2 litre ovenproof dish. Beat the egg yolks lightly in a bowl, then stir into the crumb mixture. Pour the mixture into the prepared dish and bake for 20–25 minutes until set and lightly golden on top. Remove from the oven and allow to cool slightly.

Meanwhile, make the meringue topping. Put the 150g sugar into a small, heavy-based saucepan with a little splash of water and stir over a low heat until the sugar has melted. Increase the heat and boil, without stirring, until the syrup has thickened and starts to colour very slightly at the sides. (The bubbles will get larger as the syrup thickens.) Take off the heat.

In a clean bowl, whisk the egg whites with a squeeze of lemon juice, using an electric whisk, until they form soft peaks. With the beaters at full speed, slowly pour in the hot syrup down one side of the bowl and keep whisking for about 2–3 minutes until the meringue is firm, glossy and has cooled down.

Spoon the jam over the pudding and then pipe or spoon the meringue on top. Place the pudding under a hot grill for 2–3 minutes (or wave a cook's blowtorch over the surface) until the meringue peaks are golden brown. Serve immediately.

Pears poached in perry

This is an easy yet elegant dessert that can be prepared in advance. In fact, we generally poach our pears a day ahead to give them time to macerate and take on the flavours and aromas of the spiced syrup. For a dinner party, take the pears out of the fridge as you serve your starter, and they'll be at room temperature when it's time for dessert.

Except for the pears, put all the ingredients into a saucepan in which the pears will fit snugly. Bring to a simmer and cook for 10 minutes to melt the sugar and allow the syrup to thicken slightly. (Don't worry if the perry froths up vigorously. The liquid will clear as it continues to simmer.)

Peel the pears, leaving the stalk intact, and lower them into the pan, making sure that they are covered by the syrup. Poach for 15–20 minutes until the fruit is tender when pierced with a small knife. Take the pan off the heat and transfer the cooled pears to a bowl, using a slotted spoon.

Return the pan to the heat and boil the poaching liquor steadily until it has reduced and thickened to a syrupy sauce. Pour this over the pears to coat.

Serve the pears warm or at room temperature, with vanilla ice cream or pouring cream.

SERVES 4

4 firm but ripe pears
700ml perry (pear cider)
100g caster sugar
2 cinnamon sticks
8–10 cloves
2 star anise
½ tsp black peppercorns

TO SERVE

good-quality vanilla
  ice cream or pouring
  cream

Strawberry tart

SERVES 4–6

300g sweet flan pastry
  (see page 248)
30g white chocolate,
  chopped
100ml double cream
1½–2 tbsp icing sugar,
  to taste
½ quantity pastry cream
  (see page 249)
350–400g firm but ripe
  strawberries, hulled
2 tbsp strawberry jam,
  warmed and sieved

This fantastic tart looks and tastes amazing, particularly if you use ripe, seasonal, British strawberries. It makes the ultimate end to a summer dinner party. You can bake the pastry case and make the pastry cream filling the day before, ready to assemble a couple of hours before serving.

Roll out the pastry on a lightly floured surface to a large round, the thickness of a £1 coin. Use to line a 20cm round shallow tart tin, with removable base, leaving some excess pastry overhanging the rim. Leave to rest in the fridge for 30 minutes. Melt the chocolate in a bowl set over a pan of hot water, then take off the heat and cool slightly.

Preheat the oven to 190°C/Gas 5. Line the pastry with baking paper and dried or ceramic baking beans and bake 'blind' for 15–20 minutes until the sides are set and lightly golden. Remove the paper and beans and return to the oven for another 5 minutes. Remove from the oven, and while still warm, cut off the excess pastry to level with the rim of the tin. Brush the base and sides with the melted chocolate and leave to cool and set.

For the filling, whip the cream and icing sugar together in a large bowl until just stiff. Fold through the pastry cream. Spoon the filling into the cooled pastry base and level it with a spatula.

Thinly slice the strawberries and arrange them over the filling in overlapping concentric circles. Lightly brush with the warm strawberry jam to glaze. Best served on the same day.

Basics

Chicken stock

MAKES ABOUT 1.5 LITRES
2 tbsp olive oil
1 large carrot, peeled and chopped
1 onion, peeled and chopped
2 celery sticks, trimmed and chopped
1 leek, trimmed and sliced
1 bay leaf
1 thyme sprig
3 garlic cloves, peeled
2 tbsp tomato purée
1kg raw chicken bones
about 2 litres water
sea salt and black pepper

Heat the olive oil in a stockpot. Add the vegetables, herbs and garlic and sauté over a medium heat until the vegetables are golden. Stir in the tomato purée and cook for another minute.

Add the chicken bones and then pour in enough cold water to cover, about 2 litres. Season lightly with salt and pepper. Bring to the boil and skim off any scum that rises to the surface. Reduce the heat and leave to simmer gently for 1 hour.

Let the stock stand for a few minutes to cool slightly, before passing through a fine sieve into a bowl. Leave to cool. Either refrigerate and use within 5 days, or freeze the stock in convenient portions for up to 3 months.

Brown chicken stock First roast the chicken bones in a roasting tin at 200°C/Gas 6 for 20 minutes, then continue as above. This stock has a greater depth of flavour than ordinary chicken stock.

Vegetable stock

MAKES ABOUT 1.5 LITRES
3 onions, peeled and roughly chopped
1 leek, trimmed and roughly chopped
2 celery sticks, trimmed and roughly chopped
6 carrots, peeled and roughly chopped
1 head of garlic, halved horizontally
1 tsp white peppercorns
1 bay leaf
about 2 litres water
bouquet garni (few sprigs each of thyme,
  basil, tarragon, coriander and parsley,
  tied together)
200ml dry white wine
sea salt and black pepper

Put the vegetables, garlic, peppercorns and bay leaf into a stockpot and pour on enough cold water to cover them, about 2 litres. Bring to the boil, lower the heat to a simmer and cook gently for 20 minutes. Remove the pan from the heat and add the bouquet garni, wine and a little seasoning. Give the stock a stir and leave to cool completely.

If you have time, chill the stock overnight before straining. Pass it through a fine sieve into a bowl. Refrigerate and use within 5 days, or freeze in smaller amounts for up to 3 months.

Court bouillon

MAKES ABOUT 1.5 LITRES
1 leek, trimmed and chopped
1 carrot, peeled and chopped
½ celery stick, chopped
1 onion, peeled and quartered
bouquet garni (few sprigs each of thyme,
    tarragon and parsley, tied together)
¼ tsp white peppercorns
1 tsp rock salt
½ lemon, sliced
100ml dry white wine
1.5 litres water

Place all the ingredients in a medium saucepan and bring to the boil. Reduce the heat, cover and simmer for about 30 minutes. Strain the liquid through a fine sieve into a bowl or measuring jug, discarding the vegetables and flavourings.

Use the court bouillon as a poaching liquor for delicate fish and shellfish.

Beef or veal stock

MAKES ABOUT 1.5 LITRES
1.5 kg beef or veal marrow bones,
  chopped into 5–6cm pieces
2 tbsp olive oil, plus extra to drizzle
2 onions, peeled
2 carrots, peeled
2 celery stalks
1 large fennel bulb, trimmed
1 tbsp tomato purée
2–2.5 litres water
100g button mushrooms
1 bay leaf
1 thyme sprig
1 tsp black peppercorns

Preheat the oven to 220°C/Gas 7. Put the meat bones into a roasting tin and drizzle with a little olive oil to coat. Roast for about an hour, turning over halfway, until evenly browned. Meanwhile, chop the vegetables into 5cm chunks.

Heat the olive oil in a large stockpot and add the onion, carrot, celery and fennel chunks. Cook over a high heat, stirring occasionally, until they are golden brown. Add the tomato purée and fry for another 2 minutes.

Add the browned bones to the pan and pour in enough cold water to cover. Bring to a simmer and skim off the froth and scum that rise to the surface. Add the mushrooms, bay leaf, thyme sprig and peppercorns. Simmer the stock for 6–8 hours until you are satisfied with the depth of flavour.

Let stand for a few minutes before passing through a fine sieve into a bowl. Leave to cool, then chill, or freeze in smaller amounts. Use fresh stock within 5 days, or keep frozen for up to 3 months.

Fish stock

MAKES ABOUT 1 LITRE

1kg white fish bones and trimmings
2 tbsp olive oil
1 small onion, peeled and chopped
½ celery stick, sliced
1 small fennel bulb, chopped
1 small leek, trimmed and sliced
sea salt and black pepper
75ml dry white wine
about 1–1.2 litres water

If using fish heads, remove the eyes and gills and wipe away any traces of blood. Heat the olive oil in a stockpot and add the onion, celery, fennel, leek and a little salt and pepper. Stir over a medium heat for 3–4 minutes until the vegetables begin to soften but not brown.

Add the wine, then the fish bones and trimmings. Pour in enough cold water to cover the ingredients and bring to the boil. Reduce the heat and simmer for 20 minutes. Remove the pan from the heat and leave to cool.

Ladle the fish stock through a fine sieve into a bowl. Refrigerate and use within 2 days, or freeze in smaller quantities for up to 3 months.

Lamb stock

MAKES ABOUT 1.2 LITRES

1kg lamb rib or neck bones, in small pieces
60ml olive oil
1 onion, peeled and chopped
2 carrots, peeled and chopped
1 celery stick, chopped
½ head of garlic, split horizontally
1½ tsp tomato purée
75ml dry white wine
about 2 litres water
1 bay leaf
few thyme sprigs
few flat-leaf parsley sprigs
1 tsp black peppercorns

Preheat the oven to 220°C/Gas 7. Spread the lamb bones out in a large roasting tin and drizzle with a little of the olive oil to coat. Roast for 45–60 minutes, turning halfway, until evenly browned.

Heat the remaining oil in a large stockpot. Add the onion, carrots, celery and garlic, and cook over a high heat, stirring occasionally, until golden brown. Add the tomato purée and cook for 2 minutes. Add the wine and let bubble until reduced by half.

Add the browned bones to the pan and pour in enough cold water to cover, about 2 litres. Bring to a simmer and skim off the froth and scum that rise to the surface. Add the herbs and peppercorns. Simmer the stock for 4–6 hours, until you are happy with the flavour.

Let stand for a few minutes before passing through a fine sieve into a bowl. Let cool, then refrigerate, or freeze in smaller amounts. Use fresh stock within 5 days, or keep frozen for up to 3 months.

Mayonnaise

MAKES ABOUT 600ML

4 large egg yolks

2 tsp white wine vinegar

2 tsp English mustard

sea salt and black pepper

600ml groundnut oil (or light olive oil)

1–2 tbsp cold water

Put the egg yolks, wine vinegar, mustard and some seasoning into a food processor and whiz until the mixture is very thick and creamy. With the motor running, slowly trickle in the oil in a steady stream through the funnel. Blend in the cold water to help stabilize the emulsion. Check the seasoning.

Transfer the mayonnaise to a suitable jar, cover and refrigerate for up to 3 days.

Lemon and tarragon hollandaise

MAKES ABOUT 100ML

2 large egg yolks

juice of ½ lemon, or to taste

100g chilled unsalted butter, cut into small cubes

sea salt and black pepper

handful of tarragon sprigs, leaves only, chopped

To make a water bath, bring a 3cm depth of water to the boil in a large, heavy-based saucepan. Put the egg yolks in a heatproof pudding basin with a little of the lemon juice, a cube of butter and some seasoning. Set the bowl over the pan of hot water and reduce the heat to a low simmer. Whisk the mixture until very thick and creamy, then beat in another cube of butter.

Continue beating, adding the butter a cube at a time, as the previous one has almost melted. Slide the pan off the heat if at any stage the water starts to get too hot. Once you have added all the butter, continue to beat until the sauce is thick enough to leave a trail across the surface when the spoon is drawn across it.

Lift the bowl off the hot water bath. Season the hollandaise with salt, pepper and lemon juice to taste. If it is very thick, add a tiny splash of cold water and mix well. Fold in the chopped tarragon to serve.

If not serving immediately, keep the hollandaise warm in a hot water bath off the heat and give it a stir every once in a while.

Red onion marmalade

MAKES 250ML
25g butter
500g red onions, halved and sliced
1½ tbsp light soft brown sugar
250ml dry red wine
3 tbsp red wine vinegar
sea salt and black pepper

Melt the butter in a medium pan and add the onions and sugar. Stir frequently over a medium-high heat until the onions are soft and slightly caramelized. This may take 10–15 minutes.

Add the red wine and wine vinegar to the pan and scrape up the sediment from the base of the pan with a wooden spoon to deglaze. Let the liquid bubble until it has reduced right down and the pan is quite dry. The onions should be very soft. Season well with salt and pepper.

If not serving immediately, pot the red onion marmalade in a sterilized jar and seal while still hot. Delicious with pâtés and cheese tarts.

Roast potatoes

SERVES 4–6
1.2kg floury potatoes, such as King Edward
100g duck fat or olive oil
1 tbsp plain flour
few rosemary or thyme sprigs (optional)

Preheat the oven to 200°C/Gas 6. Peel the potatoes and cut into large chunks. Add them to a pan of cold salted water, bring to the boil and parboil for 5 minutes.

Meanwhile, put the duck fat into a sturdy roasting tin and place in the oven to heat. Tip the potatoes into a colander to drain and give them a gentle shake to fluff up the sides. Sprinkle with the flour and give another few shakes to coat evenly.

Take the roasting tin out of the oven and carefully add the potatoes to the hot fat, along with the herb sprigs, if using. Toss the potatoes gently to ensure an even coating of fat and spread them out in a single layer.

Roast for 40–45 minutes, or until golden brown and crisp, turning them every 15 minutes or so, to ensure they colour evenly. Pat with kitchen paper to remove excess fat. Serve piping hot.

Yorkshire puddings

MAKES 6 LARGE PUDDINGS

150g plain flour
½ tsp fine sea salt
2 large eggs
150ml whole milk
2 tbsp beef dripping or vegetable oil

Blend the flour, salt, eggs and milk in a blender or food processor for a few minutes until smooth, stopping and scraping down the sides of the bowl after a minute. Pour the batter into a jug and chill until ready to cook.

Preheat the oven to 200°C/Gas 6. Spoon the fat into the moulds of a 6-hole muffin tin and place in the oven for 5–10 minutes or until it is really hot. Take out the tin and quickly pour in the batter to three-quarters fill the moulds. Bake for 25–30 minutes until the batter has risen dramatically and is deep golden and crisp. Serve hot.

Shortcrust pastry

MAKES ABOUT 350G

200g plain flour
¼ tsp fine sea salt
100g cold unsalted butter, cut into small cubes
3–4 tbsp ice-cold water

Put the flour and salt into a food processor. Add the butter and whiz for 10 seconds or until the mixture resembles coarse breadcrumbs. Tip into a bowl. Add 3 tbsp water and mix with a butter knife until the dough just comes together. If it seems too dry, add a little extra water, but try not to make the dough too wet.

Lightly knead the dough into a smooth ball, wrap in cling film and leave to rest in the fridge for at least 30 minutes before rolling out.

Sweet flan pastry

MAKES ABOUT 500G

125g unsalted butter, softened to room
  temperature
90g caster sugar
1 large egg
250g plain flour
1 tbsp ice-cold water (if needed)

Place the butter and sugar in a food processor and whiz until just combined. Add the egg and whiz for 30 seconds. Tip in the flour and process for a few seconds until the dough just comes together. (Do not over-process or it will become tough.) Add a little cold water if the dough seems too dry.

Knead the dough lightly on a floured surface and shape into a flat disc. Wrap in cling film and chill for 30 minutes before rolling out.

Custard

MAKES ABOUT 600ML
250ml whole milk
250ml double cream
50g caster sugar
1 vanilla pod, split lengthways
6 large egg yolks

Heat the milk, cream and 1 tbsp sugar in a heavy-based saucepan. Scrape out the seeds from the vanilla pod and add them to the pan with the pod.

Beat the egg yolks and remaining sugar together in a bowl. When the creamy milk is about to boil, take off the heat and gradually pour onto the yolk mixture, whisking continuously.

Strain the mixture through a sieve into a clean pan. Stir over a low heat until the custard thickens enough to thinly coat the back of a spoon. Take off the heat and strain through a fine sieve. Leave to cool, stirring occasionally to prevent a skin forming.

Pastry cream

MAKES ABOUT 650ML
350ml whole milk
150ml double cream
75g caster sugar
1 vanilla pod, split lengthways
  (or 1 tsp vanilla extract)
6 large egg yolks
40g cornflour

Put the milk, cream and 1 tbsp sugar into a heavy-based saucepan over a low heat. Scrape out the seeds from the vanilla pod and add them to the pan with the pod (or add the vanilla extract). Slowly bring to a simmer.

Meanwhile, beat the egg yolks and remaining sugar together in a bowl. Whisk in the cornflour, a third at a time, keeping the mixture smooth.

When the creamy milk is about to boil, slowly trickle it onto the egg mixture, whisking all the time. Strain the mixture back into the pan and return to a gentle heat. Stir continuously until the mixture is thick and smooth, but take care not to let it get too hot or it will curdle. The pastry cream is thick enough when you can draw a line across the bottom of the pan with a wooden spoon.

Strain through a fine sieve into a wide bowl. As it cools, give the pastry cream an occasional stir to prevent a skin forming on the surface. Use at once, or chill and use within 3 days.

Index